We Named Her

Faith

How We Became a
Gospel-Centered
Family

By Tim Orr

Table of Contents

Introduction to the Book

This is a book I have wanted to write for some time. I knew one day it would be written, but wasn't sure when. My wife, Michelle, suggested I write it shortly after my daughter Faith was born, but I thought at the time that it was too soon. Now the time seems right as we move into a new phase of Faith's development looking at how far she has come and anticipating her bright future.

In the fall of 2014, I put aside work on my doctoral final project and decided it was time to write the book. Quite frankly, I was burned out doing academic writing and wanted to write something that came from the heart. So I sat down one day and wrote nearly one chapter. Once finished, I printed out what I had written and asked my wife to read it. She loved it. That day, I officially began the book.

Looking back, it is amazing the experiences that life will bring. Some of those experiences are memorable like the moment of your first kiss, the time you buy your first home, or the moments you welcome your children to this world. Other experiences are far more mundane like the daily routine of going to work or maintaining household responsibilities.

The sum total of our experiences link together like a chain and make up this thing we call "life." It starts when we are born, dependent on our parents, then proceeds to unfold year by year culminating in one final experience called... death. Some people live long lives, while others live shorter ones, but in light of eternity, all lives are short in comparison. It is often said that life is but a vapor in the sea of eternity. We get only one chance to live life, so it's best to make the most of it while we are here.

All of our life experiences combine to form a story. In this book, I tell the story of our family which includes our beautiful baby girl, adopted at birth, who happens to have Down syndrome. We named her Faith.

The plan for us to adopt Faith was planned out by God before the creation of the world, and He orchestrated the necessary events to assure that Faith would be our daughter. He also orchestrated events, or at the very least, allowed them to happen, to mold Michelle and me into the parents He wanted us to be for Faith. The events God allowed in our lives shaped us into the people we are now, echoing the remarks of John Piper when he states,

> *Since God is sovereign, and this world is his,*
> *then every moment, in a sense, is a moment of*
> *providence. Wherever you find yourself right*

now has come by the process of events he ordained. Every past moment of your life has led to your now. The same will be true tonight, and tomorrow, and ten years in the future. Our experience of providence is our experience of the present, which we know has been wondrously woven together by God[1]

While Faith's story is compelling in itself, I want share how God has guided our personal experiences every step of the way to prepare us to be Faith's parents. We hope our story will inspire you as it reveals the very hand of God orchestrating events serving His purposes and displaying His glory.

Before I introduce Faith and share how we became a gospel-centered family, it is important that I outline what the term gospel-centered really means, starting with the term gospel. The gospel refers to the historical life, death, burial, and resurrection of Jesus Christ. The gospel shows how Jesus came into this world to save sinners like you and me. You will often hear the gospel called the good news because that is exactly what it is, good news for us! It's good news that we are rescued from the penalty and power of sin so we can be in right relationship with God, live victoriously, and one day begin eternal life in heaven.

---

[1] Parnell, Jonathan, "God Will Fulfill His Purpose for You," *Desiring God*, 14 December 2014, http://www.desiringgod.org/blog/posts/god-will-fulfill-his-purpose-for-you accessed on March 9, 2015

Once we have accepted what Christ has done for us, we are made new creatures in Christ. This means that our lives are changed and continue to be changed as Christ works in our hearts. People who come to believe in the gospel and turn their lives over to Christ will often hear others say that they are completely different. They don't do the same things or go to the same places any more. They are new. This is no coincidence. The Scripture declares that the old will pass away when we accept Christ.

The gospel not only rescues people from the penalty of sin, making us in right relationship with God, but also rescues from the power of sin and its hold in our lives. According to Tim Keller, well known pastor and apologist, sin's effect has psychological, social, and physical consequences.[2] I have personally witnessed God change the psychological effects of shame and guilt and replace them with a deep sense of peace and love in my heart as my sins have been forgiven. The social effects of sin which alienated me from right relationships because of my pride and selfishness were replaced with humility and other centeredness. Although the physical consequences of sin in this world and my body are evident, especially as I get older, the gospel offers me hope of life that goes beyond this world.

If eternal life and freedom from sin weren't enough, I would like to quote the marketing genius, Ron Popeil, "But wait, there's more!" The good news of the gospel means that

---

[2] Tim Keller. *Center Church: Doing Balanced, Gospel-Centered Ministry in your City.* (Grand Rapids: Zondervan Press) 34

we can live victoriously and begin the benefits of our eternal life even today. Leslie Newbigin, theologian and missionary, has aptly said, "The Christian story provides us with such a set of lenses, not something for us to look at, but for us to look through."[3] When I came to Christ, I was saved from a life that was muddled in fear, alcoholism, and ongoing suicidal thoughts. That all changed when I asked Christ to forgive me of my sins and come into my heart. I saw life differently and was able to live it differently once I understood and believed what Christ had done for me.

Later, when I married my wife, Michelle, I decided to look at marriage through the lens of the gospel. I discovered that the gospel offered a template as to how Michelle and I were to relate to one another as husband and wife. How Christ relates to His Church was to be my example.

I also discovered that as a result of regeneration, Michelle and I have the power of the Holy Spirit to live faithfully as a husband and wife. I explored this truth by asking some pertinent questions. If Christ could be raised from the dead, what did that mean as we related to one another? How could I as a man continually draw on God's resources to be the husband He has called me to be without falling back on my own performance and power? Through the gospel I have a wealth of resources and help through the power of the Holy Spirit to do so.

---

[3] Ibid. *46*

Then, sixteen years after we married, that same lens shaped the way I looked at family life as I began to raise my daughter. I found that the gospel has something to say as to how I was to raise my daughter. This book is written not to prove a theological point, but rather to illustrate that point through a story inspired and orchestrated by God. Without question, we were transformed and became a gospel-centered family.

Acknowledgements

I could not have written this book without my wonderful wife, Michelle. She has been by my side as my greatest encourager for almost twenty-two years now. She is my best friend, and I am so thrilled to be on this journey with her. At the beginning of this writing process, we thought that Michelle and I would be co-authors of the book, but her work schedule did not allow for the time necessary to invest in it. She did, however, write a draft of chapter three and managed to comb through the entire manuscript, attempting to fix any mistakes and add her perspective to several of the anecdotes included in the book. I couldn't be happier with our collaboration on this book and in our family.

I also want to acknowledge my precious daughter, Faith. I have been given the privilege of not only being her father but also writing about the little girl I love so much. God has used her to bring more joy to our already happy home in ways we never imagined!

I feel that I must give thanks to all the staff at the schools and agencies that played a part in Faith's development.

- *A Step Ahead*. Denise Cox and Lisa Wagers.
- *Parkside Elementary School*. Emily Baker, Wyn Barnette, Mona McClellan, and Becky Monroe.
- *Columbus Christian School*. Ron Bridgewater, Dorene Bowman, Tammy Harvey, Angie Herron, Pam Rogers, Kendal Wildey, and Lori Williams.
- *Taylorsville Elementary School*. Hannah Burke, Dori Hall Clapp, Pam Florence, Sydell Gant, Hana Hoffman, Colleen Hughes, Jenny Kessler, Kim Martin, Theresa Shelly, Phebe West, Allison Wilson, and Casey Voelz.

Last, but certainly not least, I want to thank the many people who read chapters of the manuscript and offered suggestions and feedback. Special thanks go out to Stephen Aryee, Annette Ballard, Randy Ballard, Harold Cooper, Terry Dibble, Katy Dutton, Melissa Eads, Mike Engelstad, Jodi Engelstad, Tony Hayes, Heather Kelley, Derek Kiesler, Jenni Kiesler, Sydell Gant, Cynthia Gover, Sharon Henderson, Mark Miller, Adrienne Mormino, Jesse Viola, Tim Viola, and Andromeda Yancey. Your feedback and encouragement were invaluable!

Chapter 1

My Name is Faith:
A personal word from my daughter

My name is Faith Orr and I am five years-old. I live with my mommy and daddy, but I have been told that I was adopted right after I was born. This means that the people I call my parents are not the ones that gave birth to me. I sure feel like they are, though, because they sure love me a lot. Maybe when I get older I will learn more about my birth family. I am so thankful for them. They loved me enough to put me with my adoptive parents.

I really love my home. It is filled with laughter, hugs, books, and tender loving care.

Everyday my mom gets me ready for school and my daddy drops me off and picks me up. We have a routine. Each day when he picks me up he asks me about what I did in school. I usually give him the same answer. I tell him how much fun I had and what I did that day, especially how many books I read.

Even though all the words don't come out right, he always seems to understand what I am saying.

I have a routine with my mommy, too. When I hear her put the key into the door to unlock it when she gets home from work, I run to the door and yell, "Mommy!", as soon as she opens it. She always gives me a big hug and smile as soon as she sees me. We spend the rest of the day together doing so many cool things. I love her so much!

School is awesome, too. I am learning so many new things. I know all of my letters and some of my numbers and can even read a few words. Mommy was even surprised the other day when I was counting with her by tens and Daddy was shocked when I counted to thirty.

School is a little hard for me, though. Since I have Down syndrome, it is difficult for me to keep up with the rest of my friends in class. I know what I want to communicate, but it doesn't always come out right. This makes me sad sometimes, but I have so many people in my life to encourage me. That helps a lot. I sure do my best to keep up. I have great parents and some really great teachers who have loved me and helped me along the way.

Mommy and Daddy say that I am ahead of the other kids in some ways, which makes me feel good. Daddy says I have the type of personality that many people are drawn to. He might be right. It seems like I have a whole lot of friends.

At home, learning is a way of life. Even though we play a lot, it seems like I spend as much time learning as playing.

Books are a big part of our family. Everyone is reading all of the time, especially my daddy. Learning is just something we do as a family.

What I like best about our family is that we try to keep Jesus as the center of our lives. I am just getting to know Him and learn about Him each day, especially right before we go to bed. Mommy will read something, and she and Daddy will pray with me before I go night, night.

I am excited about everything there is to learn and do and can't wait to see what is next for my journey with Mommy and Daddy.

My daddy told me one time that there were a lot of things that had to happen long ago before I became part of their family. He hasn't told me the story until now. Won't you sit down with me and listen to my daddy explain how we became a family, or what Daddy calls a gospel-centered family?

Chapter 2

Tim's Story

B efore I became Faith's father, I had the blessing of learning about God's providence. For more than half of my forty-six years on this earth, I have been a Christian. In these twenty-five years, I have had the opportunity to learn a lot about myself. As I look back, I can see God's hand working in my life, molding me into the person I am today.

The Day I was Born

Early in 1968 my mom discovered that she was pregnant with her first child. Judging from the Chicago Bears t-shirt that I am wearing in one of my baby pictures, my dad thought he would raise me to be a sports fan like himself. My family and extended family were elated when they found out my mom was pregnant. Three of my grandmother's sisters welcomed grandsons all within a year as well, so it was a time of rejoicing for everyone.

At the time, my mother was unaware that an operation and some medicine she took would change the course of my life, even before I was born, a fact not discovered until the day she gave birth. I was born with three birth defects. I had a cleft lip, cleft palate and a webbed left hand. Medical technology had yet to advance to the level that it is today. Consequently, there was no way of knowing that I had these birth defects until my mom gave birth to me.

After a long and difficult labor, I finally arrived. It was a rough pregnancy complete with multiple bouts of morning sickness, so my mom was glad I showed up when I did. When I was delivered, the doctor decided not to allow my mom to see me immediately. He felt that the shock of seeing her new son with the multiple birth defects might be too much given the long, painful experience of giving birth she just had endured. Instead, the doctor decided my mom needed to rest and he would discuss the matter with her later. She spent all night not knowing what happened to me. Instead, she lay in her bed wondering if I was okay and what I looked like.

Unfortunately, the doctor failed to tell my pediatrician, Dr. Scully, his decision not to tell my mom right away. He had thus assumed my mom already knew about the birth defects. The next day when Dr. Scully found out that my mom was unaware of my condition, he realized what a shock seeing my birth defects may be to my mom. He decided to bring in photos of me to show my mom the birth defects. This way it would ease her into understanding what had happened. For the first time, my mom saw her first born son with his cleft lip, cleft palate and webbed fingers. By showing her the pictures first, it allowed her to digest what had happened. Then the nurse brought me to her, and she welcomed me with open arms.

Later, during the first visit to Dr. Scully, my mom asked him about what kinds of protective care I would need based upon the diagnosis. The advice he gave played a very significant role in my life that positively shaped it for the years following. He told her to treat me like any other kid and not to overprotect me. His words meant so much. What he told my mom in essence was not to set limits for me, but let me discover my own limits, if there were to be any. I am passing on the same advice forty years later to my own daughter, Faith. Because someone allowed me to do so, I knew that she should also be free to discover those limits herself.

The Surgeries

The initial introduction to this life was a bit rough. Due to my cleft palate, I had to be fed through a lamb's nipple after I was born. Unfortunately, food routinely came out my nostrils, which was a sign of tough days ahead. While still in the hospital, my parents were told that I would have to endure several operations, and the doctors needed to get started right away. Eight weeks after I was born, I had my first surgery. During the next five years, I had eight more surgeries on my mouth and hand. By my mom's count, I went on to have nearly twenty surgeries altogether by the time I turned seventeen.

Some people might say that children who endure trauma are too young to understand, so traumatic events shouldn't have a prolonged effect. While the child may not have the brain development to accurately interpret the events, this doesn't mean that the trauma isn't real to the child, or the child won't experience any lingering effects. It's just the ability to cope with such struggles has not developed yet.

Summertime Blues

After I started school, I began to have my surgeries in the summertime. This resulted in a love/hate relationship with summer. After all, children attend school nine months out of the year and summertime is their reward. This is why, as a child, one always looks forward to this time of the year because it means unobstructed playtime. There are no schedules to keep and you don't have to get up early to go to school.

After breakfast, the kids where I lived went outside to play and didn't come back inside until nearly dark. My day usually consisted of playing outside with my brother, playing basketball with my friends, and riding my bike beyond the geographical boundaries that my mom had set. These were fun times, especially picking blackberries with my brother and being rewarded for our labor with piping hot blackberry cobbler and a scoop of ice cream. It truly doesn't get any better than that.

Yet, this only defined part of my summer. Each summer, like clockwork, I had to have another surgery. I would go in to have the surgery, stay at the hospital for a week or two to endure shots, hourly interruptions from the nurses so they could do their duties, and early wakeup calls, only then go home with my face usually still swollen from the operation. This made it difficult for me to go outside and play with my friends, knowing the inevitable questions would arise. Questions like "Why do you look like you do?", or, "Did you just get in a fight?" I never got used to those questions and they seemed to cut me deep inside. While I loved summertime, I simultaneously disliked it because I knew what was ahead.

Since the surgeries frightened me so much, I didn't like to go to the hospital. There was something about being in the hospital that struck fear, even when I wasn't the patient. When I did go in for surgery, there were two things that instilled in me a level of fear that was almost unbearable. This first was the shot they gave me while they were prepping me for surgery. The nurse gave me this shot right before the person arrived who was assigned to wheel me to the operating room. There were times before several of my surgeries when the doctors and nurses had to hold me down, so the nurse could give me the shot. The fear consumed me. Many times, in tears, I begged my mom and doctor not to give me the shot, but it had to be done. From the vantage point of a nine-year-old boy this seemed, at the time, immense cruelty.

The same level of fear overcame me whenever I entered the operating room lying on the bed, staring at the lights, with the medicinal smell of alcohol lingering in the air. This aroma triggered something in my mind which caused me to grip the sheets beside me and clutch them with all my might. I didn't understand my fear at the time, but the smell of alcohol caused me to hearken back in my mind to previous surgeries I had experienced. I intuitively knew that when I woke from the surgery the experience was going to be painful. I knew difficult times were ahead and the smell of alcohol subconsciously warned me ahead of time. Since these hospital experiences happened yearly, it created deep traumatic experiences for me as a young boy.

The nurses were wonderful, to be sure, but were of little comfort to a boy whose heart was consumed with fear. These experiences, I believe, created neurotic emotions that God later healed. In all this, God had a plan. He was there. He looked upon these events knowing what was ahead. He didn't prevent, but He did protect. He gave fortitude. He didn't act because He knew the trauma would one day be healed, allowing Him to be glorified. I also believe He was developing something in me to make me a uniquely designed father for Faith.

During this period in my life there were three most memorable traumatic events. The first one is when I was about ten years old and the doctors decided to perform an abbey flap procedure to reconstruct my upper lip. The procedure called for my lips to be sewn shut for a few weeks, which meant I was fed through a syringe, undergoing a steady diet of cheese soup and milkshakes, among other foods. There was a downside to this sort of diet to be sure, as the food I was eating was not enough to maintain my weight according to the doctor's approval. So the doctors suggested that my mom include other ingredients in the shakes to increase my caloric intake, leading me to gain some weight after about a week.

The physical toll of the procedure was miniscule compared to the emotional toll. Having to play with friends, while talking out of the corner of my mouth, would prove to be much more damaging to me. Kids made fun me because I was not able to speak correctly, which reinforced my feelings of alienation and despair. Feelings of self-hatred also began to emerge for the first time. Even though I was only ten, I had begun to hate myself and developed feelings of embarrassment because of the way I looked. I now knew more than ever that I was different. Kids seemed to remind me of that on a daily basis.

Basketball became my coping mechanism, and I resolved to become good at it. I practiced for hours and hours to hone my skills, playing several hours of pickup games at the park during the spring, summer, and fall months, even continuing that commitment in the local gym when the weather got colder in the winter. I was driven to be the best. From March to November you would find me either shooting baskets on my own or playing in a pickup game with my friends. As I became one of the best players at my school, this sport provided the avenue for social acceptance that I needed at the time. Once the kids saw me play on the playground, the snide comments turned into admiration and the other kids wanted me to play on their team. This ability to play and perform well was to become my primary source of self-worth.

Another unfortunate childhood experience came by way of being in the burn unit following one of my operations. I shared the room with a teenager, who, at the time, was a few years older than I was and was burned over much of his body. One night a team of three nurses came to give him a bath and redress his wounds. To shield me from seeing what was taking place, one of the nurses pulled the curtains shut tightly. Regrettably, the curtains couldn't shield me from the screams the teenage boy let out as the nurses administered care to his wounds. I could only imagine what was taking place. It terrified me as I was lying just a few feet away, alone, in the dark, hearing everything that was going on.

Still lying in my bed, I reacted by squeezing the blankets that were draped over me as I was trying to deal with what was taking place. Then suddenly, one of the nurses had to leave the bedside of the young man and attend to something else in the next room. When she did, she pulled the curtain back a little wider than she should have, and I saw that young man's burned body. It was too much to process at my young age. As she pulled the curtain back to shut it, I closed my eyes as tightly as I could in an attempt to remove the horrible images from my mind. The screams that I heard coming from the young man next to me, coupled with the images I saw, bothered me all night. I tried to erase the images from my mind, but couldn't. This experience troubled me for years.

I had more surgeries after that, as I continued my yearly trips to Riley Hospital to be operated on. Six years later, with my last operation I endured a medical procedure that proved to be the most physically painful of them all. In order to give me an overbite, the doctors intentionally broke my jaw then reset it and wired my jaws shut for weeks so I could get the overbite that I needed. Some of the food choices I used for my first procedure I would use again. It was back to milkshakes and cheese soup among a few other options.

After I recovered from this surgery, the doctors asked me if I wanted them to perform anymore surgeries. They felt there were a few cosmetic corrections they still needed to make. Since I was seventeen, I was now old enough to decide for myself. I informed my mom and my doctor that the procedure that they had just performed would be my last. I just couldn't endure any more surgeries. I was glad I made the decision I did then, and have no regrets today for not continuing to have the cosmetic work done.

Family Life

The hospital experiences were only a portion of the negative experiences that shaped my early life. My dad was a selfish man, a fact that many people who knew him would confirm to me over and over again through the years. Sadly, he was brought up in an unfortunate situation. His mother developed mental illness when he was a boy and treated him badly. Many times she called the police because she felt her husband, my grandfather, was trying to kill her. After a while, the cops caught on and knew my grandmother had problems. She later spent her life institutionalized and in a nursing home, having to be medicated for her illness.

After witnessing and experiencing this mental illness take place for years, my grandmother's paranoia was transferred to my father and he later exhibited similar characteristics, though much less acute. The trauma wielded on my dad caused by her Schizophrenia affected him the rest of his life. Already a natural introvert, these experiences caused him to be the most emotionally distant person many people had ever met.

His selfishness was evidenced by the fact that he repeatedly stayed home to fish as I lay in a hospital bed recovering from surgery after surgery. Instead of making the journey to Indianapolis to visit me at the hospital he found other things he needed to do. Of all the surgeries, he never darkened the door of my hospital room even one time. I really needed him, but he was nowhere to be found. I never could figure this out. My mom covered for him, trying to shield me from the rejection, usually explaining that he had to work and couldn't come to visit.

You can imagine if he were this kind of father, what kind of husband he was. His anger and rage were illustrated many times as he physically beat my mom, often leaving her face black and blue. Enduring abuse like this couldn't go on forever. When I was about five-years-old, the conflict between my mom and dad escalated to the point that my mom finally decided to move out. I recall the frantic screaming that night. I am not sure of the time, but I know it had to be late given that everyone else's lights were turned off in our subdivision. During this domestic brouhaha my mom was also feverishly putting our clothes into black garbage bags as she was moving toward making her get-away. At that point she had had enough. That would be the last night my family and I would sleep under the same roof. At the age of five, my life had changed forever.

Dealing with the trauma of surgeries and their consequences at the age of five, I also had to then grapple with divorce. My mom did her best, but she was also saddled with some problems. There was no sense of security in my life as the typical support structures simply weren't there. I lacked the secure environment when both parents were present. Due to their divorce, my home now consisted of my mom and brother as well as my grandparents. We moved in with them right after my parents were separated. This move provided stability for us during the year we lived with them.

I Have a New Dad

My mom married my stepdad, whom she met at work, a year later when I was six years old, less than a year after my mom's divorce. At first I accepted him as a father figure, but after a while I began to reject him. My mom, dreaming of a happy family, wanted my brother and me to call him dad. This just didn't sit well with me. After all, I already had a dad. Why did I need another one? I often asked myself. But my mom persisted which caused me to push back even more against her wishes.

Over the next six years, my step dad served as my father figure five days a week while I was able to visit my real dad on the other two days.

Later, my stepdad began to resent me because I resisted my mom and his request to call him dad. This resentment surfaced when we worked in the garage together. He often made fun of me and called me stupid, exposing some of his anger toward me. I realized his resentment especially in light of how he accepted my compliant brother. He was younger and happy to acquiesce to my mom's familial wishes. I, the non-compliant first born, reaped the consequences of not going along with the plan.

I am sure things were hard on my stepfather, as well. Early on in their marriage, he decided to quit his good paying job and start his own car cleaning business. He went into this new business venture with his best friend who worked with him at the time. He wasn't aware that his friend was having an affair with my mother. This relationship went on for nearly a decade, resulting in my mom having a child by the co-worker several years later. Now, as I mention these things about my mom, I must also add that she, too, became a Christian later and God changed her life around, pointing to how faith in Jesus Christ can change a life.

Four years after the affair began, when I was twelve, my mom and stepdad finally divorced. We were back living with my grandmother, who now was a widow, having lost grandpa a few years before.

About a year later, when I was about thirteen years old, my mom and stepdad reunited, except this time they weren't married, opting to live together instead. This went on for a few more years. Then, one day, when I was about fifteen years old, he came home to tell my mom that he had been seeing his former ex-wife and they were getting back together. I will never forget that day as he looked me in the eye and asked me to forgive him. I saw the despair which displayed his inner struggle of just wanting happiness. He knew what he was doing wasn't right, and part of me didn't blame him, while the other part of me resented him deeply. His departure took place shortly before my relationship with my real dad was permanently severed. I couldn't do it at the time, but I would later forgive my step-dad and ask for his forgiveness for my attitude toward him.

Right about that same time, on a cool fall day, I was waiting for my real dad to pick me up and take me to his house for the weekend along with my brother who was two years younger. When my dad arrived, I told him that I didn't want to go with him that weekend, and wasn't sure if I wanted to visit him anymore. He took this as a cue that he didn't have to fulfill his weekend duty to pick my brother and me up anymore. Several times over the previous years, my dad told my brother and me that he wished he had never gotten married or had kids. Now, it seemed that the second part of that wish had come true. The sense of rejection he must have felt when I told him I wasn't sure I wanted to go with him anymore caused a painful and distant father-son relationship for the rest of our lives.

My Battle with Alcohol

At fifteen years old, shortly after my dad and step dad walked out of my life, I was a young man who was hurting and consumed by self-loathing, anger and rebellion. The years of childhood trauma and family instability really began to take its toll. Two problems began to surface, namely my battle with alcohol and my battle with suicide.

My battle with alcohol began at a friend's house one wintery Saturday afternoon. He and I were talking in his room, probably about girls. We were having a good time, when he told me about his mom and dad's liquor cabinet located in his basement. He and I jointly decided to venture downstairs and sneak a drink. However, when I took my first drink, something magical happened. The pain, anger and bitterness that stemmed from a life of rejection vanished instantly. One drink turned into two, and two turned into four and so on. This was the first of many such experiences. It was like my problems instantly melted away.

A life of drinking was something I swore to myself I would never do. I never wanted to be like my father, who was an alcoholic. In spite of that, my life seemed to reflect the 70's classic song by Harry Chapin titled *Cats in the Cradle*. This 1974 classic was first inspired by Chapin's wife but also reflected, according to Chapin, his relationship with his son. The song details a first person account of a father who was too busy for his son. The father promises the son that he will spend time with him one day in the future. However, the son starts to mimic his father's behavior declaring, "I am going to be just like you, Dad. I am going to be just like you." In a real sense, I had begun to live out my own *Cats in the Cradle* scenario. I too had become just like my father. I had become someone I swore I would never be: an alcoholic.

Showing off my Drinking Skills

My motivation to drink was more than just to escape. It also brought me a real sense of esteem, along with my basketball skills, as I quickly developed the reputation of someone who could consume a lot of beer. This brought me false feelings of significance. People admired me for how much I could "hold my liquor" so to speak. I later found this to be a lie that at times was even life threatening.

I vividly remember visiting a friend who attended a nearby junior college. When my other friends and I arrived from Terre Haute, he introduced us to some friends he met at a party. I quickly scanned the room to find the right girl to hit on. However, it didn't take long to find out that college girls weren't interested in high school juniors. So I moved on to my first love, drinking. This gave me a great opportunity to show off to everyone my drinking skills, including the ladies.

I met a sophomore the guys called T.A., appropriately named after the *Trans Am* he drove. T. A. was also known for his ability to consume alcohol, but evidently not for his academic prowess. As we interacted, he didn't seem to have the qualities one would associate with a successful student.

He seemed to be someone who majored in partying and lived off his parents' dime. My friend posed to me a drinking challenge against his friend T. A. We played a drinking game called "quarters", a game that consists of a shot glass and a quarter with a lot of beer. Each time the opponent is able to bounce a quarter off the table into the glass, the other person has to drink.

T. A. and I played this game for probably over an hour until his eyes glazed over and he proceeded to release the breakfast and lunch he ate earlier that day all over the floor. I, at the time a high school junior, was declared the winner of a drinking game against a college guy who was known for his ability to drink. My love for alcohol not only helped me escape from the pain I was feeling, but also enhanced my social status a bit. This experience encouraged me to show off my talents at other parties.

A few months later, this new found talent nearly killed me. I received another challenge, this time from a guy named Larry. My friends were bragging about me at the party, and issued a challenge to anyone who wanted to take me on. Larry, my same age and known for his ability to consume a large amount of alcohol as well, answered the challenge.

He and I squared off in a one-on-one battle of quarters. Since I had already been drinking a bit, my confidence was high. I boldly asserted that I would assume the challenge against Larry, except I said I would drink whiskey while he drank beer. This was a huge mistake. He was not only good at drinking but had also honed his craft at playing quarters. After several shots of whiskey in a row, I collapsed on the floor. I was out cold.

My friends carried me into the bedroom and laid me down in the bed. They were worried and a few of them wondered if they should call an ambulance since it seemed that my breathing had slowed dramatically. Fearful of getting in trouble, they decided against calling an ambulance and took their chances that I would wake up fine the next morning. Fortunately for me, their bet paid off. I was fine the next day, but there was no way to test my blood alcohol level. It had to have been very high, and I am surprised I survived the experience, after hearing what had happened. Unfortunately, this experience failed to put a damper on my lifestyle. By this time, my alcohol addiction had a firm grip hold on my life.

Suicide

The life of alcoholism was coupled with an obsession over suicide. I was consumed by pain and self-loathing and often day dreamed about killing myself. During my senior year in high school I came dangerously close to following through with the plan I contemplated nearly every day. I had moved to Terre Haute from West Terre Haute the year before, but wanted to spend my final year at West Vigo High School so I could play basketball, as this was still a major source of esteem for me. In order to do so, my friend talked his parents into allowing me to move in with them for the entire school year. They took me in, and my friend John and I stayed in his basement.

Since the age of nine, I had dreamed of playing varsity basketball. Now, having achieved this goal, I realized that playing on the team wouldn't fill the longing in my heart to take away the pain and loneliness. So one evening while I was alone in the house and really battling thoughts of suicide, I remembered that John's dad kept a gun in the cabinet in the kitchen. I slowly walked up the stairs thinking that this was the day that I could be put out of my misery. I finally arrived in the kitchen and opened up the cabinet door. I was crying and wanting things just to end. I felt I couldn't take it anymore. I put the barrel of the gun to my temple, but just couldn't seem to pull the trigger. Stemming from the little religious training I had, thoughts of my eternal destiny flashed through my mind. I was told a few years earlier that anyone who committed suicide would spend eternity in hell. This was the only thing that kept me from pulling the trigger that night.

I slowly put the gun back in the cabinet and proceeded back to my bedroom. I lay on the bed, clutching the pillow as tightly as I could, crying for an hour, wanting the pain to go away. The sorrow and pain were so great. At the time, I couldn't see that God, through His sovereign grace, kept me alive that night. God had plans for me that included being a husband and a father. God would turn all these sorrows and pains to joy one day; I just hadn't realized it yet.

Since I was still ignorant of God's plan for me, I spent the next two or three years trying to drink away the pain. Such pursuits caused me to become increasingly isolated. The shame, guilt, and fear only intensified, which fed the need to drink even more.

After graduation, my drinking led me into legal trouble. Shortly after finishing school, I was arrested for trespassing at eighteen years old. The next time, a year later, I was arrested for minor consumption.

The minor consumption charge was the result of a long night of drinking. Toward the end of that evening, I decided to get something to eat at a drive-through. While waiting on my order, a security guard walked beside my car and noticed I was holding a beer and asked me to pull my car to the side. I reluctantly cooperated. He called the police and I was arrested for public intoxication, a minor offense, considering what he could have arrested me for. I received a slap on the wrist, was told not to do it again, and served six months' probation.

I failed to learn my lesson and was arrested the following year. By now I was twenty years old. This time I faced more severe charges during an experience that would turn out to be life changing. My friends and I went out partying, drinking a lot of beer and smoking a lot of marijuana one night. After we finished, I got into my truck to drive home. I felt it was safe, given that I lived only two blocks away. After driving a block or so, I passed out at the wheel and totaled two parked cars. Upon impact, I woke up not recognizing what had happened. After a moment or two I realized I had wrecked my car. Fear began to engulf my soul because I didn't know if I had hurt anyone or not. I panicked, got out of the car, and ran back to my friend's house, tripping and falling along the way.

When I arrived at his house, I told him what had happened. He advised me to lay low and stay at his house until I sobered up the next day, then report my car stolen. There was something in me that couldn't do that. Still worrying that I might have hurt someone, my guilt drove me to see what had happened. I walked back to the scene of the accident and saw my truck and the two cars I had totaled from a distance. I also heard sirens sounding off, as the police were looking for me. I rushed back to my friend's house. He again advised me to follow the plan to sober up and report the car stolen the next morning. I just couldn't do it. We waited for an hour or two and my friend drove me to my house.

My grandmother answered the door, and immediately asked what I had done. She informed me that the police had been by looking for me. Instantly I panicked, riddled with guilt for what I had done and called the police to come back and get me. A few minutes later, squad cars showed up at my grandmother's doorstep. The first officer who entered the house drew his handcuffs and handcuffed me in my grandmother's living room. Then, along with the other officers, he escorted me outside, put me in a squad car and took me to jail. Despite the embarrassment, I was happy that no one was hurt due to my poor judgment.

Because of this incident I received one year probation during which time I would need to see a probation officer and drug and alcohol counselor. God used this occurrence to eventually bring me to faith.

However, despite probation, I still risked going to jail for a drink. Blinded by my addiction, I was unable to see what I was doing to myself until one of my monthly visits to the drug and alcohol counselor. As I sat down in the chair across from him, he began to ask me the usual questions: How was I doing? How was everything going? After a few minutes of chit chat, he asked me if I had stayed sober since I last saw him. As always during these visits I lied and told him I had not taken a drink. But this time he kept prodding me, and I finally admitted that I had continued drinking.

Immediately he asked me if I was an alcoholic. I responded by telling him, "Absolutely not!"

Not missing a beat, he responded back saying, "Usually people who are not alcoholic won't risk a year in jail for a drink."

That statement was like a dagger driven into my heart. God used that statement to expose my sin and self-delusion. The counselor followed up by encouraging me to attend an A.A. meeting, which I did.

I nervously went to a meeting the next day expecting to see a bunch of old men with gray beards. Lo and behold, that is exactly what I saw. But something happened that night that had never happened before. I heard people share their stories and I realized that they thought and felt like I did. That was the first time I ever felt like someone understood me and what I was going through. After the meeting one gentleman came over to me, knowing that I was much younger than anyone else, and suggested that I attend another meeting on the other side of town. He told me that many of the people who attended that meeting were much younger.

After attending the meeting at the new location, I engaged in a conversation with someone who later became my sponsor. While leaving, I noticed a poster on the wall that read *The 12 Steps of Alcoholics Anonymous*. As I glanced at each of the steps, one of them seemed to leap off the poster. It was the third step that states, "Made a decision to turn our will and our lives over to the care of God as we understood Him." I thought about that statement all the way home.

When I arrived home, I turned on the TV out of boredom. As I was flipping through the channels, I stopped on the channel that aired the 700 Club. As I listened, Pat Robertson was speaking and it was like he was speaking to me personally. That night, through the magic of TV, he led me to Christ. I would never be the same. God, as I had understood Him, had always been the Christian God. My understanding, however, was skewed, having not understood a key element of the Christian message. I believed in God and believed in Jesus to be sure, but never understood the gospel. It wasn't that I didn't know about the sinner's prayer or had never heard about getting saved. I learned those concepts by occasionally attending my grandmother's church when I was a kid. Several times, I had answered altar calls and repeated the sinner's prayer. I understood that Jesus forgave past sins, but never understood the concept of justification.

In retrospect, I now know that I really never understood the gospel. After I answered each altar call before, I got up from my knees and tried to be a good person. Each time, I had relied on my works to save me. But that night, something different took place. God cut through my misunderstanding and illuminated the gospel to my heart by His Holy Spirit, which allowed me to grasp what Christ had done for me.

What I discovered that night, in its full orbed reality, was that God came to save sinners.

As a result of putting my faith and trust in Christ, my sins were forgiven: past, present, and future. The gospel, as I discovered, is the good news of the death, burial, and resurrection of Christ. Through these acts, I was justified in the court of heaven. While I deserved eternal punishment, through Christ's death on the cross, He took upon Himself the punishment of my sin. My conversion came as a result of placing my faith in the finished work of Christ alone for my salvation. I was delivered from both the power and penalty of sin. I had become a new person.

This didn't mean, however, that I ceased to struggle with sin. It was just that now I had victory over it as I surrendered each area of my life to Christ. This required that I grow deeper and deeper in my understanding of the gospel. I found that with God, through the assistance of the Holy Spirit, coupled with the study and meditation of God's Word, this could take place. As a result of this pursuit, my heart and mind began to change.

The burden of the guilt of my sin rolled away. Fear was now dispelled from my heart. I understood how much God loved me. I didn't have to try to earn His approval. He was no longer the traffic cop in the sky. Instead, God became my loving Heavenly Father. The more that I understood how much I had been forgiven the more I understood His love. For nearly twenty years I grew in my understanding of His grace before Faith entered my life.

After my Conversion

Two years after my conversion, I began to feel the call to serve in full-time ministry. I believed I was destined to be a pastor. So, to prepare, I went off to a small Christian college in Cleveland, TN named Lee College. During one of the convocation services they held each semester, the minister preached on Joel and God's promise to restore everything the locusts of sin had eaten. I embraced that promise as my own. For me, the locusts of sin were represented by a high divorce rate in my family, so part of that promise for me, I believed at the time, was to give me a godly wife, whom I would marry a year or so later. Another part of that promise was to give me children, which I now know was to be our beautiful daughter. However, this was all very confusing after I later found out Michelle and I probably would not be able to have kids. The latter fulfillment would not take place until several years later. Until then, I would continue to grow in the grace and knowledge of Christ.

It wouldn't be until we adopted Faith, that I realized how my understanding of the gospel would transform my parenting. This transformation took time, however. Early in my conversion, I filtered every experience through the lens of a damaged self-worth, which affected my total life experience. Though I knew my salvation was secure, doubt and fear still dominated my thinking. However, over time, I began to comprehend the grace, acceptance, and love God has extended to me through His Son.

Christianity teaches that everyone is equally unrighteous and condemned before God if one has not accepted God's free gift of salvation. The person who lived a good life prior to conversion was just as condemned before God as the person who was a prostitute in the streets of LA. With that said, I think the person who has lived a sinful lifestyle may have a greater capacity to understand the forgiveness that Jesus brings. This is certainly what I believe happened to me. As the saying goes, those people who have been forgiven much will love much, and may have the capacity to love in a more unconditional way. Because of my sinful past and difficult childhood, I am a better father than if my experience would have been different. This may not be true for everybody, but it was certainly true for me.

What I Learned

After my conversion, I was determined to be the best father and husband I could be. I didn't want to make the same mistakes I saw growing up. So the sixteen years leading to adopting

Faith after Michelle and I were married, prepared me to be a better parent.

First, I learned God puts people in families. Until my conversion, I never really thought about nor cared much about family. I was someone who really only cared about himself.

Granted, I loved my mom and dad, as well as my brothers and sister, but we were never close. Because of our own personal family breakdown, my friends served in that role, while my family served a subordinate role as a sort of extended family.

Through the miracle of procreation, every human being gains a family. After all, by God's design, it takes a mother and a father to have kids. So when I converted to Christianity, I began to read the Bible and discover what it says about this important relationship. My salvation experience instilled in me a desire to have a wife and kids.

My family life took a different turn than expected as I adopted instead of having my own biological child. Later, I would discover that a family who chooses to adopt takes a different route but arrives at the same place. God, through His sovereign grace, allows families to adopt. For my wife and me, God placed Faith in our family to give us the opportunity to nurture her spiritually and emotionally. Faith was ours, and I was determined to train her in the ways of God so she could one day experience the salvation that Michelle and I had experienced.

Second, I learned that to be an effective Christian parent, I must know God as well as experience the transforming power of His Word in my life. When God gave me the promise about turning around what the locust of sin had eaten, I began to seek Him even more. The more God transformed my life, the more I could later nurture the spiritual life in my daughter. As a father, I am to teach my child to be devoted to God. The Scripture calls believers to love God with all their heart, mind, soul, and strength. As I walk with God, I am to continually cultivate a heart increasingly devoted to God, then transfer the value of having a prayerful and devotional life to my daughter. But it first has to start in me.

Third, I learned to show Faith the love and forgiveness I received from God. Through the gospel, God bestowed His love and forgiveness on me. Shortly after Michelle and I married, we attended a conference with Archibald Hart. He talked about the importance of a good theology of ministry, which he took from the first few chapters of 2 Corinthians. This part of the chapter had the most impact on me: "Blessed be the God and Father of our Lord Jesus Christ, the Father of mercies and God of all comfort, who comforts us in our affliction, so that we may be able to comfort those who are in any affliction, with the comfort with which we ourselves are comforted by God." (2 Cor. 1:3-4, ESV) Basically the verse calls believers to minister to people in the same way God ministers His love and grace to them.

When applied to the father/daughter relationship, I as a father am to draw from my relationship with my Heavenly Father so I can be a good earthly father to my daughter. Nothing could bring me greater joy than to know that I am bringing God's grace and love to Faith. It is worth all the hardship and heartache I went through and will continue to impact Faith her whole life.

Chapter 3

Michelle's Story

If one desires an understanding of God's design for wife, Genesis 2:18 is the place to start. The verse declares, "Then the Lord God said, 'It is not good that man should be alone; I will make him a helper fit for him.'" After nearly twenty-two years of marriage, my wife lives out this admonition as well as any woman I know. My love for her has grown over the years, and she has truly become my very best friend. I love her today more deeply than I did when we first got married.

I am delighted to share how God formed her into the person she is today. God prepared her first to be His daughter but has also shaped her into the wife she is to me and the mom she is to Faith.

Michelle was born in early September 1966 as the first-born to a teenage couple who had not even graduated high school yet. Michelle's father did the noble thing and married her mother once they realized Michelle's mom was pregnant.

The odds were stacked against her parents for marrying at such a young age. Her mom was sixteen years old when she became pregnant. Like any other teenager in that predicament, Michelle's mom had the difficult task of telling her traditional parents that she was pregnant.

One can only imagine what went through their minds when they found out the news. The sixteen year-old daughter who had just learned how to drive, who was still in high school, who had nearly three years left of her teenage years would now be a mom. To them, she was still their little girl. Now she would have a little girl of her own. They were quite disappointed to hear the news.

You have probably heard stories, like I have, of situations like this where parents have sent their daughter out of town to live with relatives to save the child and family the embarrassment, especially in those days. Michelle's grandparents would have none of that.

Instead, they stood by Michelle's mom and helped her plan a wedding, and even helped with childcare which says a lot about how much they loved their daughter.

Maybe her grandparents intuitively understood how she would respond. After Michelle was born her mom decided she would go back to high school to get her diploma. This was unheard of in her small community, a young girl known to have a baby returning to high school. Nevertheless, her mom went to the superintendent's office to inform him of her plan. He was not pleased, but something about her mother's fortitude convinced him that it would be best to let her have her way.

Getting pregnant is one of the leading reasons why teenagers drop out of high school today. Demands of motherhood become far too great. Getting up in the middle of the night to feed the baby, changing the diapers several times a day, and catering to the newborn's every need is taxing. It is much easier to rely on the government or one's parents for financial stability than to pursue school. The temptation was there to be sure, but Michelle's mom had parents who steered her in a different direction.

Michelle's mom succeeded and completed her high school career when Michelle was only a year old. There is an iconic photograph of the three of them as a young family with her mom in her graduation gown on graduation day.

Michelle drew much inspiration over the years from that example. It inspired her to understand that despite obstacles she faced, she could do whatever she set her mind to do, just as her mom had done.

While her mom stayed home with Michelle, her dad worked for a car company in the factory. He had lived a hard life. The reverberations of his difficult childhood would continue throughout the entire time Michelle lived at home.

Some of Michelle's earliest memories were of her dad and his struggle with alcoholism.

For years he sought to anesthetize the memories of growing up with an abusive father. Michelle's mom shared a family story about her dad being woken up in the middle of the night to be beaten by his father. This common occurrence struck fear in her father and surely affected his self-esteem.

The alcoholism became a problem in the early part of the marriage and in turn led to other problems. Alcohol abuse often leads to issues such as anger, aggression, and irresponsibility and it certainly led to these with Michelle's dad. Sometimes the arguments between Michelle's parents would spill over far into the night which caused Michelle's mom to strongly consider leaving her dad on several occasions.

After one of those arguments, Michelle remembers her dad threaten to leave for good. At her young age, Michelle didn't understand and, not wanting to lose her dad, she began to frantically cry, telling her father that she wanted to go with him. He responded by assuring her he would take her to work with him. Even in her young mind, probably around five years old, she knew he would never be able to follow through on such promises and realized he had a problem.

The effects of growing up in an abusive home plagued her father for years. It caused him to have some difficult issues especially in securing and keeping work. Because of this, Michelle grew up feeling insecure about money. Her parents always made sure they had food and shelter, but she knew they weren't like the other families at her school as most other fathers held steady jobs. Later, this caused her to be overly concerned with her own job security. While it has made her an excellent worker, she still monitors the temptation of letting the drive for security lead to letting her job take too much of her personal life.

Fortunately, Michelle's father's early problems lessened with time. After the death of a dear friend in a car accident due to consumption of alcohol, he quit drinking completely. Michelle shares that she felt he always loved her and would do anything for his kids. He still dealt with financial issues, but family life greatly improved once he was able to give up drinking.

Michelle remembers her family being a happy one, relatively speaking, as they worked out problems and grew together. Her parents went on to have two more children, her sister, Roberta, and her brother, Bob. Despite having to live on public assistance for much of her childhood, they developed a happy family together.

Michelle often tells people how powerful my testimony is, having come out of the lifestyle that I did. But I really think Michelle has a more powerful testimony. I was exposed to Christianity at a very young age, but never followed through with a commitment to Christ. God had to bring me through many trying circumstances to get me to the place where I surrendered to Him. For Michelle, this wasn't the case.

At a young age Michelle was drawn to Jesus. Thanks to the love and prayers of her grandmother, she was introduced to Him and His church at a young age. Her earliest memory of church is when she was around five years old, walking down the rickety stairs of her grandmother's church to the basement for Sunday school class. As Michelle walked into the room she instantly noticed the other children all sitting on rough-hewn benches, listening intently to the teacher.

Even though the basement smelled old, she didn't mind because she was so mesmerized by what she saw. The children were led to stand and sing "Jesus Loves Me". When she heard the children singing all around her, she suddenly felt God's presence fill the room, and fell in love with this novel, amazing experience. Not really understanding it, she still enjoyed the fellowship with the other children. Even at her young age, the music impacted her deeply, the lyrics staying with her long after she left that day.

Moving Closer to Home

When Michelle was around ten years old, her father gained employment with the oil rigs in Michigan. She still vividly remembers when her parents came home with a carload full of goodies, including new bikes and a color TV. It was like Christmas in July! This seemed to be a new beginning for the family.

Around this time, her parents decided to move closer to Michelle's grandparents, a move that would prove life-changing for Michelle. Fortunately, her grandmother took it upon herself to regularly take her to a small Free Methodist church, the same congregation as the one she visited as a child, but now in a new location. Michelle's grandmother went on to make the single greatest impact upon her life, serving as her first spiritual mentor.

Through this relationship, Michelle continued to develop an understanding of God's character, but still hadn't accepted Jesus as her Savior. At the age of twelve, that changed when she headed to summer church camp with her grandmother. During one of the evening services, she responded to the invitation to surrender her life to Christ, deciding to accept Him as Lord and Savior. She went to the altar and prayed that God would forgive her sins and told Him that she now chose to live for Him. Michelle recalls leaving that service and walking back to the campsite feeling as though she were a new creation, with her grandmother walking by her side, glowing with happiness at the commitment Michelle had just made.

After that, Michelle sought to live out the Christian life as best she could but didn't enjoy the luxury of living in a Christian home. Without her parents as Christian examples, she didn't understand how to really live a transformed life. Luckily, her grandmother assisted her when she could. No doubt, God strategically placed Michelle's grandmother in her life to fulfill a discipleship role. Michelle believes that God orchestrated events five years earlier to compel her parents to move back closer to home so her grandmother could play this all important role in her life.

A Changed Home

Two years later, the spiritual temperature in Michelle's home changed, as her mother made a commitment for Christ when Michelle was fourteen years old. Instead of being happy about it, recalls Michelle, she was scared because now she would have to get serious about following Jesus, too. However, those fears eased as she realized that as her mother lived a Christian life, it would become easier for Michelle to be in God's word and live out her faith.

During this same time, her father seemed to have changed as well, having stopped drinking earlier and now quitting smoking, things that Michelle never thought he would do. Now their family was stable and moving forward.

When Michelle turned sixteen, one of her Christian friends invited Michelle to work the summer with her at Spring Hill Camps in Evart, MI. This was a wonderful experience for her as she met other young Christians who were zealous for God. She spent time praying and seeking God unlike she had ever done before. God used this experience to help Michelle draw closer to Him and understand how to live for Him with the power of the Holy Spirit as her source.

The Big Decision

During her senior year, Michelle made a decision that affected her future. Most of the people she grew up with didn't want to move away and decided not to go to college. Instead, they got married shortly after high school. Such an arrangement didn't allow for the time to receive a university education or work a higher paying job.

Her decision centered on a boy she dated in high school, a relationship that became pretty serious during her senior year of high school. Her boyfriend was a sweet person, but she knew he wasn't the man God had for her. He even asked Michelle to marry him, but she said no. As Michelle looks back at this experience, she knows that she was not prepared to start a life with someone at that time because she wanted to go to college and explore all the interests she had cultivated in high school such as art and music.

While Michelle felt sad that she had disappointed her boyfriend, this experience helped her get a little closer to knowing what she wanted in life and what God had in mind. She knew that it was time for her to move away from home and see what was next for her.

The College Years

After Michelle graduated from high school at the age of seventeen, she attended a small evangelical Christian college, called Spring Arbor College. This decision came as result of a series of divinely orchestrated events that helped serve God's divine purposes. She had attempted to save money and go to a small community college near her home, but the dean of admissions at Spring Arbor College called and asked what was keeping her from attending his school. She told him it was a money issue. The Dean responded by helping Michelle accept some scholarships and loans, literally coming to her home, helping pack her stuff in his car and taking her to Spring Arbor College a few weeks into the first semester of classes. While it seemed rather extravagant, Michelle felt a peace about the move and knew this was the right thing for her to do.

Attending Spring Arbor College enabled her to experience Christian fellowship with other young people her age. It gave her a spiritual foundation that would have been lacking had she continued to attend the community college. It also allowed her to make important choices about her career in a Christian environment.

In college Michelle was surprised to find that many of her friends were preparing to marry, a longstanding tradition in most Christian colleges. A few even revealed that their purpose in attending a Christian school was to get their "MRS" degree. This was a totally new concept for her. She had the idea that college was preparation for a career, not marriage. Even so, until then, she hadn't really thought about the qualities that would make the perfect mate. While she didn't intend to use college to get her MRS degree, she realized that it would be wise to think more seriously about this issue. Michelle had crushes on different young men before and even dated a little but still did not find anyone she could seriously consider for marriage. As a result of her experiences and study of God's word, she knew that she wanted a man serious about his relationship with God, committed to being a leader in the home, and passionate about ministry.

While Michelle appreciated the amazing experiences she had at Spring Arbor College, she realized that she would have to pay off some pretty hefty loans since it was a private school. During a summer job near her home, she started looking at other options for her college career. After two years at Spring Arbor, Michelle decided to transfer to Central Michigan University. She also decided changed her major from flute performance to Spanish after a class trip she had taken to Mexico.

Central Michigan appealed to her because the school offered an interesting degree in Bilingual Education which seemed to fit everything Michelle wanted to do. The desire to reach out cross-culturally was being kindled in her heart. Once she decided to attend CMU, she found a place to stay in Mt. Pleasant and started classes pursuing her love for Spanish and education.

God was clearly directing her path. At CMU, Michelle connected with a high school friend, Tamara, the one who had invited her to work at Spring Hill Camps a few summers earlier. Tamara invited Michelle to her Christian fellowship group, something very important on a secular campus, which offered the opportunity to bond with some Christian friends who would greatly impact her life. Her faith grew immensely in this group and seemed to be the next step after the solid spiritual foundation God had developed in her at Spring Arbor.

In all of this Michelle continued her pursuit of learning and mastering the Spanish language, took two more trips to Mexico and learned much about the needs of second language learners in her courses. While attending CMU, she discovered she had the gift for teaching. She had no idea that her most important student would be born several years in the future. However, once Faith was born Michelle realized that God had been preparing her through those early experiences to be Faith's mom and first teacher.

Her love for teaching carried over into her church life as she volunteered to teach middle school Sunday school class at church. Although scared at first, Michelle soon realized that she enjoyed thinking of creative ways to teach the kids and help them understand the gospel at their impressionable age. One of her greatest gifts as a teacher is creativity.

Another aspect of life at CMU that prepared Michelle for God's purpose for her was meeting and living with Bertha. She was an elderly lady in the community who needed someone to stay with her, making sure she had meals and was generally cared for. A nurse came in to help her with baths, but Michelle did most other duties. Bertha was not known for her kindness or patience, but God gave Michelle the grace to love her and pray for her as she entered her final years.

Michelle's Christian friends also impacted her. On Friday nights, the fellowship group met at Bertha's home. They sang music, discussed Scripture, and built up one another's faith. After each meeting was over, they all gathered for informal fellowship.

After the school year finished, Michelle left for a trip to Mexico while a friend from her fellowship group stayed with

Bertha. As the summer progressed, the two often ate together and had long talks which often included spiritual conversations. During one of those conversations, Bertha was curious about the Christian faith and asked Michelle's friend a lot of questions. Eventually, her friend asked Bertha if she would like to accept Christ as her Savior, which she did. Michelle was thrilled to get this report from her friend and humbled to have played a small role in Bertha's conversion. After a semester of seeing the gospel lived out amongst Michelle and her friends, plus her friend's evangelistic heart all worked together to cause Bertha to be ready to receive the gospel message and make a decision for Christ.

Michelle Enters the Workforce

After college, Michelle took a job teaching English as a Second Language in Houston, Texas, far away from her home state of Michigan. Unfortunately, she was lonely there because it just didn't feel like home. She stayed there for one school year, but because of the distance decided to move as close as she could to her family, having become very homesick.

After searching for a job closer to home, Michelle finally found one in Marshall, IL, eight hours from family and just seventeen short miles from her future husband. When Michelle arrived there, she decided to go to the same church denomination she had found in Texas, having liked the freedom of worship and good Bible teaching. She called the pastor of the church in Terre Haute, IN, and asked about the church and its services. Little did she know she was speaking to the pastor who would eventually marry us, Randy Ballard. Michelle has never forgotten that first conversation and when she hung up the phone, she just knew that this was going to be the church for her.

Children Appear on the Radar

Michelle was so busy with her college life and beginning a career that thoughts of children were far from her mind. However, this all changed when her brother had a son while she was living in Marshall. Michelle loved being an aunt to her new little nephew, and this began to stir the desire for motherhood. She realized that one day she might have children, too.

She wondered what her children would look like. Would they have that classic family nose and chin that was handed down from generation to generation? Would she be a good mom? Her expectations were much different than the future reality, but God often does that. He will not always use conventional means to accomplish His purposes. After all, He used a young virgin girl to be the mother of our Savior, a 100 year-old man to be the father of the faith, a renegade Pharisee to write two-thirds of the New Testament. All were unexpected, unorthodox means accomplishing God's purposes and ensuring that God gets the glory and not man.

Looking back over all these experiences beginning in her childhood through early womanhood, Michelle realized that God was preparing her to be, first and foremost, His daughter.

In order to truly develop her into a strong daughter of His, she needed to develop a strong devotional life. To achieve this, God orchestrated events to place Michelle in different relationships and experiences that strengthened her relationship to Christ. God used her grandmother in her life to serve as her spiritual mentor. She showed Michelle how to have a strong relationship with Christ, knowing that, without one, she would have nothing to bring to anyone else. God orchestrated all of this first of all because He wanted Michelle for His own, but also because Faith needed a mother who knew God and could gently lead her to Him.

To grow into the person God wanted, Michelle had to conquer some obstacles along the way. God gave Michelle her mother as an example of someone who overcame the obstacles teen pregnancy can bring and still graduated with her high school diploma. This experience inspired Michelle to achieve the academic training needed to be a teacher, never giving up on her dreams. This steadfastness is an essential element that she has passed on to Faith to help her overcome intellectual hurdles. Her patience and love for teaching and learning has helped her minister to Faith, resulting in strong gains in all areas of Faith's life.

Even in the difficult childhood experiences with her father, God was preparing her for motherhood. He showed Michelle how to be loyal, patient and loving to those God brings into your life. Someone's beginning does not determine how they will end. Her father had a tough life, but overcame many difficulties.

One of the best gifts her earthly father gave her was that she always knew that he loved her. For that reason it was not a difficult leap to believe that her heavenly Father loved her as well. Because of this Michelle understands that she can teach Faith about God's love through example and understanding.

Finally, by watching how God changed Bertha, Michelle witnessed the power of the gospel to change someone else's life. She realized that people need exposure to Christians living out the gospel in authentic, loving ways. Each time Bertha heard her friends singing, laughing, talking about Jesus, she was getting closer to becoming His child. This instilled in Michelle a commitment to live a gospel-centered life, which she would later pass on to Faith.

Chapter 4

Heartbroken

The ups and downs of life were revealed to us early in our marriage. Our story begins with Michelle and me meeting at church during the fall of 1990, shortly after she arrived in the Terre Haute, Indiana area. The year before, she had become a bilingual teacher after graduating from Central Michigan University, where she began her teaching career in Houston. Since the distance between Texas and her home state of Michigan was so great, she decided to try to find a job closer to home. Marshall, Illinois, became the closest possibility.

Not finding her preferred denomination in this small country town, she ventured over to nearby Terre Haute and found one. Randy Ballard served as their pastor and he, along with his wife Annette, would make the single greatest impact on our Christian lives. Without a doubt, choosing this church was a divinely orchestrated decision.

When I say Michelle and I met at the aforementioned church, we were more like acquaintances. Sure, we said, "hi" to one another from time to time, but that was about the extent of it. When we met, I was a recent convert to Christianity, having been saved out of a life ravaged by alcoholism. At the time, God still needed to do so much more in my life, things I will explain in upcoming chapters. Being socially awkward, I didn't interact with people much at church, at least for the first couple of years I was there. Terrified to talk to anyone, I desperately wanted someone to talk to me. I would often sit in the pew until church started hoping someone would approach me to talk and, invariably, someone would.

I had always struggled with this social awkwardness. Before my conversion, I needed to have a drink to be able to functional socially. It took a few years to get to the point where I could feel somewhat comfortable interacting in a room with people I didn't know very well. Because of this social disposition, I especially didn't feel comfortable interacting with the opposite sex. So, obviously, Michelle and I didn't talk or interact much, but that would soon change.

The First Date

In May of 1992, things took a radical turn. Michelle decided to ask me out. I was glad she did since I had only been on one date since my conversion three years earlier. When she did ask me, she didn't do it the traditional way. Instead, she opted to ask a friend to see if I was interested, who instead asked the pastor's wife who asked the pastor if I would go out with her. While her actions violated every dating procedure imaginable, it worked because I returned a "yes" back through that chain of communication.

When we went on our first date, once again, Michelle defied the traditional way of dating, picking me up instead of the other way around. This wasn't because she had embraced the thinking of some feminist thinker advocating the obliteration of gender roles. The reason was simple: I did not have a driver's license. A few years earlier, I had been arrested for my third offense of driving while intoxicated, minor consumption, and reckless driving. Since I had failed to do what I needed to do to get my license back, I was still without one. Michelle knew I didn't have a car, but she didn't realize I didn't have my license until after we went out to the car to begin our date. Michelle, being the traditionalist that she was, asked if I would drive because, in her family, the men always drove. I, reluctantly, had to tell her I didn't have my license, so she would have to do the driving. The look on her face was priceless! Her feeling of disbelief and her look of dismay, sprinkled with a little dose of fear, was evident. Years later, she told me the date was almost off because of my response.

Despite this rocky start, the date actually went quite well. After she picked me up, we went to the Olive Garden for dinner. I remember being nervous, not knowing what exactly to say. But the words seemed to come when I needed them, and we had a nice, polite conversation. That was our first dinner, the beginning of many Olive Garden anniversary dinners to come in the following years.

After eating, we played miniature golf while continuing our comfortable conversation. Since we hadn't talked much nearly the entire two years we knew one another, we had a lot to talk about. She shared with me where she grew up and what it was like to be a Michigander. I, in turn, shared with her my mischievous past, difficult childhood, and the dreams I had for ministry. We capped off the night with a Ferris wheel ride at the Banks of the Wabash Festival.

Despite it being a romantic evening, that night I decided this enjoyable date would be the first and last with Michelle. I didn't see any reason pursuing the relationship because I thought my future wife was back at Lee College, now Lee University, where I had just finished my first year. Now, my sights were set on finding a woman back at college.

Courtship and Marriage

After our date, Michelle went back to Michigan where she would spend the summer with her parents. Something would happen to both of us during those months, though. Michelle felt a clear leading from God that she was getting married soon. So, in response, she began, at least to a certain degree, to plan the wedding. She picked out the wedding colors and decided where the wedding would be located among other details. This, of course, made it very easy for me when we did decide to get married several months later, because all the important decisions had already been made.

I, on the other hand, had to be persuaded by everyone, from my closest friends to my pastor, that Michelle was the one for me. Because I was preparing for a future in Vocational Ministry, I assumed my "wife" was also attending Lee…although I had yet to meet her. I was relying on my own understanding at that point. Today, I feel so fortunate that God's sovereignty orchestrated the events that put Michelle and me together.

When Michelle returned from summer break a few months later, I saw her at church on Sunday. The pastor preached a message, and, to this day, I don't remember much what he said. I do, however, remember the altar call, at least the Holy Spirit's leading. I felt overwhelming confirmation in my heart that I was to marry Michelle. In hindsight, I wouldn't recommend choosing a spouse this way, but given my problems and spiritual immaturity, God chose to work in this way, nonetheless. Immediately after the service concluded, I made a beeline over to Michelle and asked her out. She graciously accepted my invitation, with her mother and grandmother listening in on our conversation. When I left, they both asked, "Who is he?" Little did they know that I would be Michelle's husband in a little under a year, and that it was the beginning of a wonderful ten month courtship that would end in a beautiful marriage.

Wedding Bells are Ringing

Since I have seen so much divorce, hurt, and pain in my family and extended family over the years, I was determined to have a great marriage and family. To prepare, Michelle and I went through three or four marriage books as well as six weeks of premarital counseling with our pastor. I wanted no stone left unturned. Together we prayed, fasted, talked, and discussed every facet of marriage ranging from sex to finances. We tried to do everything we could to prepare a happy marriage and glean the wisdom necessary to be parents, picturing our future as having the typical two wonderful kids and living in a house with the proverbial white picket fence.

The culmination of our preparation took place on June 12, 1993, when Michelle and I exchanged our wedding vows, and began our life together as husband and wife. The wedding was at a quaint little town called Barryton, Michigan, about forty minutes from Mount Pleasant, Michigan, the nearest larger town. Most of Michelle's family was there and some of my family members made the eight hour trip to see us get married. Our pastor, Randy Ballard and his wife, Annette, were also in attendance. Randy graciously presided over the service, and a wonderful one it was. The church was nearly filled as we began the service.

The ceremony was at Michelle's home church. Since Michelle and I neither one made much money at the time, we had an economically suitable wedding. Normally, the wedding reception is where the majority of the money is spent. To drastically cut costs, the church graciously catered the wedding. They did not disappoint. Several ladies from the church got together and cooked a wonderful meal, and Michelle's mom baked the wedding cake to perfection. The wedding dress was homemade, but looked like a dress one would buy at an expensive store. We felt so blessed.

At the wedding reception, I was introduced to a tradition I never knew existed. As we were sitting at the head table, I was engaging in small talk with Michelle and suddenly noticed several people taking their spoons and tapping their glasses with them. The first time this happened, I leaned over to Michelle and asked what was happening. She informed me that this was a longstanding tradition where the people were cueing the groom to kiss the bride. I suddenly warmed up to the tradition. One of things married couples learn right away when they get married is that each spouse comes to the marriage with traditions handed down from generation to generation. So, merely an hour after we wed, I received my first lesson.

Many people that day told us how they sensed a specialness about our marriage. Everyone felt, including me, that God had His hand on our marriage. In hindsight, I think they were right. Looking back almost twenty-two years since that day, I know I married the right person for me. Since then, Michelle and I have grown closer together over the years and have become best friends.

Shortly after the wedding we departed for our honeymoon. After all, the marriage is not complete without one. As I already mentioned, we did not have much money, nor did our parents. We planned to spend a few days at Indiana Beach then go back to work. Indiana Beach was an amusement park located on beautiful Lake Shafer in Monticello, Indiana, about 3 hours southeast from where we were married. Unfortunately, the weather refused to cooperate as the forecast called for storms that week. As a result, our honeymoon was rained out. What were we to do? After all, the honeymoon is a special component of the start of a wonderful marriage. For many couples, the memories of the honeymoon are right alongside the memories of the marriage ceremony itself.

Before I share what we did on our honeymoon, I must point out that Michelle married a pastor, and a young inexperienced one at that. I had yet to pastor my first church, but I was in training. Training, research, and information gathering are pursuits that come natural to me. So, my choice regarding where to spend our honeymoon should not have come as a surprise.

My grandmother's denomination was having their annual camp meeting service, and that was the place where we spent our honeymoon. Yes, you read the last sentence correctly. We spent our honeymoon attending workshops during the day and enjoying the evening service at night.

During one of the evening sessions, Michelle and I were introducing ourselves to some of the people sitting near us. I will never forget the reaction of the person who introduced himself to Michelle and me. After exchanging a few pleasantries, I told him we were on our honeymoon. The gentleman didn't miss a beat and promptly replied, "Then, what are you doing here?" As soon as he said that, I glanced at Michelle to get her reaction. When I did, I had the strange suspicion that she might be thinking the same thing. I am sure this is not how she had planned her honeymoon would look like growing up. It took me a few trips to *Disney World* later in our marriage to make up for my mistake, which allowed the legendary Mickey Mouse to serve a redemptive purpose.

I don't want to convey that we have lived a storybook marriage. This is certainly not the case. I firmly believe there is no such thing as a perfect marriage because when two sinful people come together, there is bound to be conflict along the way, and our marriage is no different. Yet, we established strategies during our ten month courtship that helped to resolve conflict when it emerged.

While there are no perfect marriages, there are good ones and bad ones. That day was the start of a good marriage. Having earnestly done all we could do to prepare, I had to trust God to do the rest. He hasn't disappointed. God has been there when we called to Him, walked with us through the storms, and guided us to establish, not a story book marriage, but a very happy one that Michelle and I cherish.

Would we have children?

While a happy marriage was part of our immediate future, we would learn later that children were not. I do not believe that children are essential to have a happy marriage. A couple can be perfectly happy while remaining childless. However, knowing this truth failed to provide any comfort at the time. Early in our marriage, we discovered that we would not be able to have children of our own. Due to a thyroid condition, Michelle had suspected this for years, but we decided to visit the doctor after trying unsuccessfully to have children.

When we visited a doctor to get medical advice, we both nervously walked into his office. I had become somewhat content not knowing for sure if we were able to have kids because there was always the possibility we might. Now I wasn't sure if I wanted a definitive answer to our question about fertility. By not knowing what was wrong, I was able to have hope that one day we could have a child of our own. Michelle felt the same way. But, finally we determined to have the necessary tests done.

Michelle and I sat in the doctor's office waiting to hear the results. When he entered the room, there weren't any facial expressions offering a clue as to what they were. Somewhat stoic in his countenance, he sat down, eased back in his chair, opened the file and proceeded to relay to us the tests' conclusive findings. What Michelle had suspected was confirmed. The results revealed that it would be very unlikely that Michelle would bear children. The door of opportunity had now seemed to be forcefully slammed shut.

A few years earlier, during pre-marital counseling we discussed all of the intricacies of married life. We hammered out our expectations of what the husband's and wife's responsibilities were to be. We discussed the domestic responsibilities such as who would wash the dishes and who would take out the trash. We also discussed the importance of being on the same page regarding how we parent. We were evangelicals, so having kids was assumed. After one of the premarital counseling sessions, I recall sitting down with my soon-to-be wife discussing our views of parenting. We decided, to no one's surprise, that I would be the disciplinarian and Michelle would be the nurturer. Now, none of that mattered as we walked out of the doctor's office... dismayed and heartbroken.

So, early in our marriage, one of our dreams had been crushed. Having kids is part of one's dreams about marriage. At least, that was the case for us. If I were to have a son, I envisioned taking him to activities like baseball practice and pouring my heart into him so he could be the husband and father God intended him to be. I envisioned taking my daughter to dance recitals, assisting my wife in hosting slumber parties or, at least, being in the other room as my wife assumed the honors. Then, one day I would walk "my little girl" down the aisle so she could marry the man of her dreams. Michelle and I now realized that this was not going to be something we would ever experience. Fortunately, God had other plans for us.

While painful at the time, we soon learned to stuff that pain by being busy doing ministry and building careers. Ministry took our eyes off of the loss that we felt. But soon God would use this situation to serve His redemptive purposes.

74

Chapter 5

Busy Doing Ministry

G rowing up, I heard the phrase "God works in mysterious ways" countless times. People usually uttered this statement when they didn't understand why a certain situation like a job loss or the death of a relative was taking place. This was the go-to statement when something was taking place in their lives they didn't understand. The phrase suggested that God allowed something negative to happen to fulfill His mysterious purpose.

Paul and Silas

Such a statement begs the question: Why are God's ways so mysterious? In any case, His ways leave people perplexed.

In Acts 16, I am sure that Paul and Silas were asking the same question at first. Having been jailed for their faith, they were arrested then beaten. Apparently, their response to this treatment suggests they found an answer to the question of God's mysterious ways rather quickly.

On the way to a prayer meeting, while minding their own business, they met a slave girl, who was a fortune teller with a spirit of divination. She began to cry out mockingly on behalf of Paul and Silas which drew negative attention from the people. After seeing this, Paul became annoyed and cast out the demon that was motivating her to say such things. Later, her owners became enraged because the girl renounced her fortune-telling gift, which was a lucrative business for them. The owners brought in the magistrates and stirred up the crowd, leading to Paul and Silas's arrest.

Following their arrest, they were put in jail. Obviously, they were well acquainted with God's mysterious ways because they were singing and praising God in the midst of their situation. They had endured similar situations many times. During their time in jail, Paul and Silas made the most of their situation and ministered to the jailor and his family, which resulted in them coming to know Christ. God was working in a mysterious way in order to fulfill His redemption plan.

Similarly, albeit in less dramatic fashion, God worked in our situation as a result of our inability to have children and used it to serve His redemptive purpose.

God's Plan to Redeem our Situation

During the spring of 1994, Michelle and I were living in Terre Haute, preparing to serve in vocational ministry. To prepare, we were going through our denomination's Ministerial Internship Program. The internship called for us to complete reading and writing assignments as well as meet once a month with other prospective ministers. During one of those meetings, the State Overseer told the fifteen or so ministerial candidates and their wives not to expect pastoring an established church upon graduating from the program. Instead, we should set our sights on planting a church.

So, Michelle and I took what he said to heart and began praying for where God might lead us to plant. We never dreamed this new direction would take us to the place where most people would never think of planting a church.

We prayed and searched the scriptures for a few months until we were confident of God's direction. To everyone's surprise, except for my pastor, we chose the East Chicago/Gary, Indiana area to plant our first church. I still remember telling my pastor, who, at the time, also served as the state's Evangelism Director for our denomination, I wanted to plant a Hispanic church in that area. Later, the church evolved into a multicultural church with the majority of the parishioners being African American. This idea seemingly came out of nowhere. At the time, I never knew anyone who had done anything similar to what I was doing, and certainly there were almost no Hispanics in Terre Haute that would have spawned the idea. This idea seemed to be from God, and our pastor affirmed this by telling us that he felt this was from the Lord. Several months later, after much preparation, off we went, but not before some testing of our faith.

Our Faith was Tested

Fortunately, my home church invited us to participate in a church plant, which allowed us to glean some much needed experience. They had bought a building in a very needy part of Terre Haute, Indiana, in order to start a church called the Caring Center. After Randy asked me if I was willing to co-pastor the church until they found someone else to lead it, I gladly accepted the invitation. The first service had about twenty people in attendance. For the next six months I worked very hard to grow the church, along with the mother church, before I left for East Chicago. By the time I left to move to East Chicago, the new church was running sixty in attendance. I was asked if I wanted to stay and serve as pastor of this new congregation, but I turned down the invitation to begin the church in East Chicago. To me, the direction for my future seemed clear.

Even though we felt the call to plant the church in East Chicago, we had not secured jobs. Michelle would have to find a fulltime job, and I would have to secure a job as well. Since Michelle was a Spanish teacher, she needed to have a job secured prior to the beginning of the school year if we were to make the move to East Chicago.

She had filled out application after application for a job in the East Chicago/Gary, Indiana area, but to no avail. Then, one day in July, a school in Illinois, very near Chicago, called and interviewed her for a job. She and I went to the interview and were shocked by what we saw. It was the first time we had ever seen metal detectors in a high school. It was like we were entering a war zone, which, in some ways, we were. Now, we weren't ignorant that some schools needed devices like this to protect students and staff, but it was just that Michelle was coming from a small rural school, and those devices weren't needed. Luckily, the school chose someone else to fill the position.

For the next few months, we continued to wait for a school to call, watching as June turned into July and July turned into August. We had prayed and prayed about what to do because if we waited much longer, we would have had to wait another year to begin our work in East Chicago. Then, one day in prayer, God gave me an inner assurance that we were to launch out in faith. After about a week or so of deliberation, Michelle quit her job, I quit my job, and we started our adventure to our new city, still without employment. We agonized about the decision but felt like it was the right thing to do.

Then, a few days later, a school called, except this time the school was in Indiana instead of the Chicago suburbs. Either coincidentally or providentially, depending on your view of God's activity in the world, the school happened to be the school we stopped at on our way back to Terre Haute, after being interviewed by the school with the metal detectors. This new school wanted Michelle to interview for a middle school Spanish position. She responded to their call with an enthusiastic, "Yes" and, a few days later, went for an interview. The people who interviewed her liked her so much they would have hired her on the spot if she had had an Indiana license.

Just a few days before, Michelle had applied for an Indiana license. She sent in her application with the other materials that needed to go with it. Unfortunately, as we were driving home discussing how the interview went, she suddenly realized a check had been sent instead of a money order with the application. They would not accept a personal check, of course. Since she needed to get the initial okay from the state licensing board right away, this glitch would have cost her this job. Immediately after discovering Michelle had not sent the right document, I felt the Holy Spirit speak to me that the sent envelope was sitting on the secretary's desk. I haven't had an experience like that before, and not many since, but God was sovereignly guiding our steps and honoring our faith.

Few people had cell phones back then, so we stopped at a telephone booth at the local McDonald's to call the state's licensing agency. The woman who answered the phone told Michelle she was not the one who usually answered that phone but offered to help us anyway. After Michelle explained the situation, the lady informed her that the normal protocol is to send back the check. However, she said that she was the mail lady and it just so happened that Michelle's envelope was sitting on the desk in front of her. She said she would hold onto it for us. I can't express the joy we both felt at that news. We rushed to get the money order we needed and made a beeline to Indianapolis. That Monday, Michelle received a call from the school, telling her they had received initial approval from the state licensing board. They instructed her to come in and sign her contract immediately. It was amazing for us to see God work in this way!

East Chicago Experience

A week before Michelle got the job, we officially became residents of East Chicago. On a hot and humid Saturday morning, Michelle and I, together with family and friends, ventured over to our new city in a Ryder truck. The truck was packed full of furniture and books, and we all had the sore muscles to prove it.

Michelle and I decided to live in the city in which we would minister because we needed to experience exactly what our people were experiencing. Besides, White, Alienated, Separated and Protected (WASP) living arrangements didn't exactly appeal to us. So we secured a one room apartment in the main part of town. It sure wasn't an apartment that met the standards of the Lake Shore Drive clientele. Most of the apartments in this building were studios, except for the corner ones, which had one bedroom.

Fortunately, we were able to secure one of the corner apartments. However, there was no elevator service, something I failed to tell my family and friends helping me move that day. When we arrived at our new apartment, I parked the moving truck in the back, giving easy access to the stairs. When he noticed the building had three stories, my best friend, Jeff, asked me on what floor was the apartment. I told him the third floor, which was a secret until then. Jeff, as well as the other friends who traveled with us, were not amused to discover they were helping their friends move to a third floor apartment with no elevator!

Once we got the last items in the apartment, we traveled back to Terre Haute to say our goodbyes to the congregation who loved and supported us for the past five years. Michelle and I were two of the many people who had been sent out into fulltime ministry from that church.

For our final service I preached and Michelle led worship one final time. We enjoyed worshipping with the congregation that had invested in our ministry. They had watched us grow, and now we were ready to launch out and begin our new church. Following the service was a send-off party filled with love, hugs, and tears. Now it was time to discover what God had in store for us.

Introduction to a New Life

When the service and party ended, we traveled back to East Chicago that night to our new home. Arriving four hours later, we were exhausted so we immediately walked up the steps to our apartment to prepare for bed. Once inside, we laid down our bags, relieved we could finally rest and relax. It had been a long, tiring weekend!

After we opened all the windows, letting the breeze in, something happened. We heard gunfire from what seemed to be very close by. Michelle and I instantly hit the floor, scared to death! We waited for a minute or two and slowly crawled over to the couch, under the window, to check on what was happening outside. We didn't see anything. About an hour later, we built up the courage to lie down for the night. Michelle and I prayed together, asking God to calm our fears as we wondered if we had just made the biggest mistake of our lives. He, however, had us in the middle of His will, protecting us from danger every step of the way.

Our first day was quite exciting, to put it mildly. This experience confirmed that ministering effectively in our new environment would require us to live a life of faith and trust in God. The need to draw strength from Him daily had been made crystal clear. He would have to be our source, which we would find out later is a great place to be.

Shortly after that experience, the O. J. Simpson trial came to a close. O.J. Simpson was a football hero who was accused of killing his wife and a family friend. The day the police were to arrest him, he, along with a friend, took off in a white Bronco and fled. The police followed his car and the whole scene was captured on national television as people in helicopters filmed everything that was taking place. It seemed everyone in America was watching. Simpson was arrested that day and a while later stood trial.

The trial would symbolize the battle against systemic racism, a battle that people of color had been fighting against for so long. Unfortunately, this kind of racism continued to be justified by white America. Years of racism, discrimination, unfair hiring practices, and police brutality had boiled over.

African Americans were demanding justice, not just for OJ, but for all of black America. During the trial, as I went about the town, you could feel the racial tension in the air. A not guilty verdict seemed to be one way some of the injustices leveled against the African American community could be atoned.

For months this trial was debated, and it really revealed the racial divide in our country. I saw this clearly while I was sitting alone in my apartment listening to the verdict. When the not guilty verdict was read, I couldn't believe my ears. O. J. Simpson was declared not guilty?

But the reaction of the people in my apartment building and the people on the streets further shocked me. To my surprise, there was joyful exuberance at the announcement. At that point, I knew that I had a lot to learn about the culture in which I found myself.

The trial was similar to the 2014 Ferguson trial in terms of the racial tension that undergirded the case although the circumstances of the cases were quite different. In the Ferguson case, many in the African American community believed the grand jury failed to indict a guilty white police officer after he killed an unarmed black man. For most African Americans, they were reliving one more example of a system that was against them.

For the first time, my eyes were opened to the effects of racism and the deficiencies of the white church in addressing urban problems. Quite frankly, they just didn't seem to care.

Their mantra was that the welfare system had caused all the problems, and we just needed to have smaller government to solve the problems. Maybe that was partly true, but it certainly didn't tell the whole story; Michelle and I learned that sin was both personal and systemic, and everyone, no matter race and color, mattered equally to God. It was out of that commitment we began to reach out with compassion to the people in our new city.

We took this commitment to the community. My ministry focused on adults. I ministered to anyone who was receptive, whether business people, drug addicts or prostitutes. Since Jesus loved everyone, I was determined to do the same.

We also sought to reach the children of East Chicago, and my wife predominately lead in this role. As we reached out, we saw children in desperate need of Jesus' love. Before we moved to East Chicago a pastor and his wife took us around town, and we saw the graffiti, heard the stories of gang violence and the poverty driven issues. Despite the needs and problems we witnessed, we felt we were up for the challenge with God's help.

God's Redemptive Purposes

During this period of our lives, the absence of children actually helped us serve God in a way not possible otherwise. God used the inner desire to minister and make an impact on children of our own and transferred that desire to minister to the children of the community in which we were ministering. We never saw ourselves as a substitute for their parents, but we were able to give the children, to some degree, a parental role model. There were so many broken lives devastated by the effects of sin. Many of the children we ministered to were from homes where either one or both grandparents served as guardians. Many of the children clearly desired a mother and a father and seemed drawn to us in that capacity.

One child in particular, I will call her Louisa, was being raised by her grandmother. Her father, who also lived with her grandmother, was a member of a gang and she didn't have much of a relationship with her mother. Her father's gang involvement became evident to us one day when Michelle dropped her off. Michelle and I had just finished an outreach at church, so we divided up the kids and drove them home.

For Michelle, Louisa's was the last stop. When Michelle dropped her off, she immediately turned her radio on full blast, and went to Dairy Queen and bought a much-deserved ice cream treat. She didn't realize what took place at Louisa's house right after she left. Since Michelle was taking longer than I thought she should, I called Louisa's house.

When her grandmother answered the phone, we exchanged some niceties and then I asked her if Michelle had been by yet. She told me that Michelle had just left and was probably on her way back home. Then, something happened that sent fear to the deepest recesses of my heart. Over the phone I heard a car drive by and began to fire about five or six bullets at Louisa's house. I still remember hearing the "tinging" sound as the bullets hit the siding.

This was the environment in which Louisa and her family lived. This was also the environment we ministered in regularly. Fortunately, Michelle, oblivious to the whole thing, made it home safely. She was quite surprised to find me outside our apartment waiting for her. I told her what had happened and she and I both were thankful she was safe and sound.

God Loves the Little Children

The Bible teaches that Jesus loved the little children. On one occasion, people were bringing Jesus little children so He could pray and minister to their needs. Astonishingly, the disciples rebuked the people for doing it. Jesus responded to them with force stating, "Let the children come to me and do not hinder them, for to such belongs the kingdom of heaven" (Matt. 19:14).

This truth became crystallized for me one day when I went on a weekly trip to Gary, Indiana to pick up a lady named Erise with her six grandchildren. When I arrived, I walked up to the door to let them know I was there. Erise always had them ready, so I simply asked them to load up in the van, and they did. Erise said she would follow behind in a minute or two. As I led the children outside, I noticed two people from a gang with arms extended pointing guns at rival gang members, who were standing on the corner in the housing project where Erise lived. I quickly rushed the kids back in the house and called 911.

We nervously waited a few minutes until the police arrived. When I saw the squad car approaching, I signaled to the kids to load back into the van. As we walked out to the van, the squad car stopped in front Erise's house and asked me if I had called the police. I couldn't believe my ears. I thought to myself, "You have just made me a marked man."

Later that week, Erise's friend, Buddy, called to let me know the word on the street was the gang members wanted to "take me out" because some of them had been arrested. This, of course, was something you never wanted to hear. The call took place on Wednesday and I seriously debated whether I would continue to risk my life by picking up Erise and the kids.

That Saturday, my church had a children's event at one of our parishioner's homes located in Hammond, Indiana which is right next to Gary. When I arrived again at Erise's house, she and the kids were outside waiting. I parked the van and opened the door to let them in. After we left her cul de sac a car with four young men inside pulled up beside us and began yelling at me.

I immediately asked Erise, "Who are those guys?" She said, "They are part of the gang that was in the altercation a few days before which resulted in some of their friends getting arrested."

When I drove up to the next stop sign, the four young men were still driving right beside me, yelling at me the whole time. Truly, I was scared to death. I really didn't think I was going to survive. What Buddy warned me about on Wednesday seemed to be coming true now. Luckily, they were just trying to scare me and drove off. I can't tell you how relieved I was when they did.

The next day was Sunday and I was due to pick up Erise and her grandchildren for church. I woke up that morning praying and debating whether I would make my weekly trip to Gary. Finally, I decided I was not going to be intimidated, so I left the house and headed for Gary. I am glad I did. On my way over to their house, I prayed the entire time, asking God why He had called me to minister in such a dangerous place. It seemed I was making limited impact on people's lives, so why go on? The Spirit of God reassured me I was picking up Erise and her grandchildren because they mattered to Him. People matter to Him. I never forgot that. They might not matter to the people who live in the suburbs, but they do matter to God. This greatly impacted my view of ministry and reinforced our purpose for being there.

God also inspired Michelle that the children in this community mattered to Him. She assumed the role of mother on several occasions as the need to have a nurturing mother figure in the children's lives became increasingly evident. Michelle developed special curriculum for the children, had special Saturday events, and developed relationships with the children by visiting their homes and inviting them into ours whenever possible. There were children from homes that had many issues and needs, and needed patience and love during teaching. We tried our best to impact the children with the love of Jesus whenever we could.

My role in the children's ministry was to build relationships with the kids on the streets. I served as a substitute teacher, which allowed me to get to know many of them. When it was time for church or special events, I would go out to the streets and compel them to come in, helping Michelle with supervision and often opening the services with a fun chant so that children would realize this was a safe, happy place to worship.

The ministry we began in East Chicago area lasted for the next ten years. I served as pastor for five years and for another five years I served as a part-time associate pastor at two other congregations in East Chicago and Hammond. Developing a strong love for the community and believing in reaching out to families in any way we could, we learned so much about ministry during those ten years, grew in our marriage and saw people's live change before our eyes.

Conclusion

Soon, our daughter would come into our lives, but God had more to this story before the parenthood chapter could begin. God would use many more life experiences to serve His purpose and prepare us to be Faith's parents.

Chapter 6

Adoption is on our Radar

Through our experiences growing up, our courtship, marriage, and infertility, God was molding us into the parents we are today. Throwing ourselves into ministry and serving in the East Chicago area further shaped our character, preparing us spiritually and emotionally to one day take care of our little girl.

God now led us on a new adventure. After leaving East Chicago in 2005, I served as a pastor of a church in a small Southern Indiana town for two years. The church was a bit of an adjustment for me as I was far more comfortable in an urban area than a rural one. While the rural life wasn't exactly a foreign one as I had lived in a rural area for part of my childhood, it never seemed completely comfortable to me then or now. Nevertheless, Michelle and I appreciated our time there as we served the congregation with glad hearts.

Most of people in that congregation valued family very much. They valued being together to such an extent that they refused to locate to other, more economically lucrative, areas, and believed that having children was something everyone expected couples to do.

Several of the people in the congregation wondered why Michelle and I didn't have children of our own. At first, this surprised us because it wasn't a question broached during the interview process. Other than our parents hoping for grandchildren, no one had ever questioned us on the issue so we didn't really think of bringing it up. They didn't know that we had always wanted to have kids but weren't able to have any of our own for medical reasons.

One day the subject came up before a Sunday service. It was about 20 minutes before service started, and I was engaging in small talk with some of the early arrivals. As I was talking to one of the parishioners who had attended the church for several years, she asked me why Michelle and I still didn't have children. She graciously told me that we had so much to offer a child and just wondered why we hadn't had any yet. I politely told her that we were not able to. She then asked if we had considered adoption; there were so many children who needed a home.

Michelle and I had certainly thought about it. A few years earlier, we were going through the adoption process and decided that the time wasn't right to adopt. Instead we believed God would have us assume custody of Michelle's nephew for a few years. For the time being we shelved the idea of adoption.

Michelle's nephew was ten years-old when he came to live with us. He was coming from some pretty rough circumstances and we spent the next five years devoted to raising him the best we could. We offered him love, a Christian education, and a stable home environment. After five years with us he moved back to live with his mom. We loved him very much and had the opportunity to raise him for a time, but he was our nephew and not our son. Also, he longed to have the experience of living with his mom before he was completely grown up and we understood that. God had all this in mind and we now realize that our experiences with our nephew also helped prepare us to be Faith's parents.

We enjoyed serving in Bloomfield, but Michelle was not able to find a job in that area. She searched far and wide never even landing an interview. The closest place she could find a job was in Columbus, Indiana, which was a little under two hours away from my pastorate. We found ourselves living as commuters from Michelle's work to our home and church.

It May be Time to adopt a Child

Since the distance was so great and Michelle's job situation seemed indefinite, I decided to resign that pastorate two years later and we settled in Columbus, Indiana, where we currently reside. After a year there, the desire to have a child of our own reemerged. In the fall of 2008 we began the adoption process. Not really knowing what direction to take, we began sort of half-heartedly. In our minds questions lingered, causing us to hesitate a bit. For instance, did we really want to have a new-born as we began our forties? Could we really afford adoption? Fortunately, we never allowed these doubts to dominate our thinking. But they did take a small toll on our enthusiasm and the doubts affected our initial adoption attempt. However, our desire to have one last chance to pour our lives into the life of someone else was greater, so we continued our journey.

By the end of 2008, Michelle and I had begun the adoption process, where paperwork, interviews, and observations abound. We were asked many questions throughout the process. One of the questions during the initial interview was regarding what kind of baby would we would be willing to adopt. Would a child with a different cultural heritage be ok? Did the age of the child matter? How about disabilities? While the questioning was uncomfortable to us at first, we knew that it was an essential part of the process. After all, adoption situations vary, and the adoption agency needs to know if a prospective child will be a right fit for the adoptive family.

Michelle and I pondered these questions for about a week and were in joint agreement regarding our answers. We were open to any race or nationality. Given our extensive multicultural background experiences, this was a "no brainer". Concerning age, we wanted a newborn, one of our essential wants in a child. As Brooke, our adoption coordinator, reviewed the list of possibilities, we were asked about disabilities. Because of our age, having recently entered our forties, we decided against adopting a child with special needs. We would learn later, however, that God had other plans.

Christmastime

Around Christmastime, Michelle and I made our way to my mom's home to celebrate Christmas with my side of the family. When we arrived, my mom, grandmother, sister and both brothers were sitting in the living room waiting for everyone to arrive. As was our tradition, we retired to the living room as my mom, sister, and grandmother finished preparing the meal. When the meal was served, everyone gathered around the table to celebrate a nice Christmas holiday.

Later we exchanged our gifts with one another and continued to exchange pleasantries. I noticed a somber look on Michelle's face. At the time, I simply brushed it off thinking nothing of it. I found out later that Michelle was a little depressed because she was experiencing yet another childless Christmas. She felt something was missing.

Sometimes experiences like this either drive us to despair or drive us to prayer. On our way home, she presented her concerns to the Lord, explaining how much she wanted a child.

That night, she had a heavy heart, similar to that of Hannah of the Old Testament, the Prophet Samuel's mother, a story recorded in the Book of I Samuel. Hannah was barren for many years and desperately wanted a child. The inner desire to be a mother was further compounded by the fact that her culture dictated that a large family was the result of God's blessing.

I am sure she struggled with feelings of deep alienation from God given that she was not blessed by Him. To make matters even worse, her husband's other wife ridiculed her for her barren womb.

While Michelle's experience wasn't quite as drastic, many of her friends had children and were celebrating their Christmases together that day, but not her. So on the way home, unbeknownst to me, she took her situation to the Lord and prayed. In the middle of her prayer, she felt a confirmation from Him that we would have a child of our own before the following Christmas. It seemed fantastic even to her, but she felt an assurance that was unexplainable and was compelled to share her experience with me. When she got home she wrote about it in her adoption journal and forgot about it soon after. Once Faith was born, she decided to start writing in the journal again and found the entry. It was a reminder that God had not forgotten her and knew her heart's desire.

God Changes our Plans

Around April 2009, Michelle suggested we take some time in extended prayer once again on one of our trips to Michigan. Up until then the desire to adopt was half-hearted at best on my part. So we proceeded to pray as we were driving on this long trip. As we were praying, Michelle once again felt impressed by the Holy Spirit that we would have a child that year. God eventually honored her prayers. For me, it took a little longer to be convinced.

A month later, God's sovereign hand would become evident as our minds would change regarding what type of child we would be willing to adopt. I was teaching a religion course at the local university at the time, so I needed to supplement my income by substitute teaching during the day. One day in May, I accepted a two day assignment at a local elementary school. The evening before the first day, I was ill and unable to go in to work. Normally, if a substitute doesn't show up on the first day of a two day assignment, the school will find someone else to teach the second day. Fortunately, they allowed me to come to work and teach the class on that second day.

When I arrived at Parkside Elementary School, I was told my assignment was to teach the preschool special needs class, an age group I am not particularly gifted to teach. Even though one of my graduate degrees is in elementary education, the university never taught me how to teach three year-old children. Teaching adults at the university level was much more my forte. God's ways are mysterious but best! He leads us where we should go even when we are unsure.

When the students got off the bus and entered the classroom, a little girl named Lilly immediately walked up to me, tilting her head to look at the tall man in front of her. When she did, she extended her arms straight up, the universal sign to get picked up. I obliged and did just that, accepting her gracious invitation. After picking her up, we walked around the room a bit pointing out things and discussing what they were, then I put her down. When I did, she walked away, only to return and ask to be picked up again. When I did, something happened inside of me which I felt was a leading from God to adopt a child with Down syndrome, a thought I had never considered before.

Later that day, doubts began to flood my mind as I realized the possible challenges that might lie ahead. I talked to both of the teacher's assistants in that classroom and they informed me of the challenges I might face. Despite the doubts, I decided to run my thoughts by Michelle. We were down to one car that day, so I had to pick her up. As soon as there was a pause in our conversation about her day, I shared the story of my day and what happened in the classroom. I said that I thought God might be leading us to adopt a child with Down syndrome. I expected her to say something like, "We really need to think this through." However, her response was not what I expected. Immediately, she told me that what I said immediately seemed right and warmed her heart. She encouraged me to look into the matter come Monday.

A Phone Call Away

I first contacted the Department of Child and Family Services and asked if there were any children with Down syndrome who needed a home. The lady on the phone informed me that she had been in her position for several years and had never heard of a child with that particular disability be put up for adoption through her agency. She encouraged me to check with adoption agencies that specialize in that area. I wondered if this would turn out to be rather difficult to accomplish.

Later that day, I looked on the Internet and found the Down Syndrome Association of Greater Cincinnati. It is an organization that provides many different forms of support for the Down syndrome community. Their main goal is to educate people to help them keep their children born with Down syndrome. Another of those services is to help set up possible adoption relationships.

They put us in touch with a wonderful lady named Robin Steele. Robin is the founder of the National Down Syndrome Adoption Network and also was connected with the Down Syndrome Association of Greater Cincinnati. Having been one of the founding families of that institution, she is a national heroine when it comes to adopting children with Down syndrome. She has matched many children to adoptive families as well as adopting her own children with Down syndrome.

The Adoption Process Begins

When I called her one afternoon, she answered the phone and I told her that my wife and I wanted to adopt a child with Down syndrome. I could hear the excitement in her voice as she replied to my inquiry. She asked some initial questions such as where I was from and how I came to my decision to adopt. After I answered her questions, she told me that there happened to be a family in Indiana wanting to put up their child for adoption. However, as she continued I found out that there were a few caveats. The birth family wanted a family that had no other children in the home, and they wanted it to be an open adoption.

An open adoption is one in which the adoptive family and birth family maintain a cordial relationship with face-to-face visits and open contact via phone, email, etc. When Robin told me this, I was hesitant. I feared that Michelle and I might be taken advantage of or have our personal privacy violated. As we continued the conversation, I asked about the family, and Robin calmed my fears. She explained that the birth family was a delightful family that just wanted the best for their daughter. As a sense of relief came over me, she asked if I thought my wife and I wanted to pursue the possibility of adoption any further. I replied with an emphatic, "Yes!"

She explained that the birth family had a few inquiries already, but they didn't think any of the prospective adoptive parents were a right fit. I initially thought that since Michelle and I were in our forties, they might think we were not a right fit either. Those doubts did not deter us. We knew that God had a plan for our family, and we would operate on faith that we should pursue this option.

Robin explained that our next step would be to send the family a birth letter that tells who we are and why we want to adopt. We knew the response would be quick as the birth mother was late into her pregnancy and wanted to put her child up for adoption immediately after she was born.

A few days later, Michelle and I emailed Robin our letter, then we patiently waited for her response. We asked many of our Christian friends to join us in prayer. After a week or two, we assumed that the birth parents weren't interested. But shortly thereafter, we discovered that wasn't the case. They were interested!

We then took the next step of the adoption process, a conference call. After setting up a time to talk, we anxiously waited. We finally got the call and huddled around our cell phone with the speaker on so we could both hear everything. We were so excited and nervous! After we introduced ourselves, we progressed from small talk to heavier subjects.

The couple told us some of the issues the baby might be facing: heart issues and a blocked intestine that would require surgery right after birth. They also shared why they were putting up their child for adoption. That is a big question that many since have asked us. Why or how could they do this? Michelle and I do not know their struggle on this issue, but we will never forget the birth father sharing his heart about Faith's diagnosis saying, "We didn't understand why God would do this, but we knew that someone must have been praying for a child and God knew we would never abort our child."

After this hurdle, they called again, wanting to meet us in person. The arrangements were made, and they came to visit us a week later. The waiting time was difficult, yet there arose in me an increasing assurance that everything was in God's hands and that He had a plan. Michelle and I spent each night praying for God to open this door.

When the birth family finally visited us, I could hardly believe it. It was like we had known one another all of our lives. We found out that day that we had so much in common.

The birth father and I were both politically conservative and fervent I.U. basketball and Bobby Knight fans along with many more commonalities. As we continued our conversation that day, I could sense that this was really going to happen. God was going to give us a daughter.

After a few hours, Michelle and I escorted the birth family to the door to bid them farewell. As we waved goodbye, I could see from Michelle's facial expression that everything had gone well as far as she was concerned. I felt the same. We were hopeful we would hear news right away that they had chosen us to be the birth family.

We were nervous when a few days turned into a week or two, and we hadn't heard anything. On that first Sunday, I remember going to the altar at Randy and Annette's church and having them pray for us. When I did, I couldn't stop sobbing. It was almost uncontrollable as the burden to pray had overwhelmed me. As a result of responding to this burden, the Holy Spirit gave an incredible assurance that we would have a daughter soon. Michelle, kneeling right next to me, felt the same way.

A few days later, around nine or ten o'clock in the morning, we received a call from the birth family asking us if we would be willing to raise their daughter as our own. We had to restrain ourselves from bellowing out our excitement while on the phone, but when we hung up we jumped for joy, clutching one another tightly. What I had been promised in the college chapel years ago about how God would return everything the locusts had eaten now would be even further fulfilled. I would be a father and Michelle would be a mother. That night we called our parents and they rejoiced with us.

Now Michelle's nesting instincts kicked in full force. We painted the living room, dining room and baby room all within a week or two. We knew we were having a girl so pink and yellow filled her new little room. Since she was due in a matter of weeks, baby showers shortly followed, five in all. Some had to wait until after she was born, but we appreciated each one. We often joke that people must have taken pity on us starting so late on our parenthood journey. The generosity of our family, friends, and church family overwhelmed us.

We faced one of our most important decisions: what would we name our daughter? Even before she was born, we felt a deep connection with her and prayed for her and all she would face as she came into this world. Michelle and I kicked around many names we found online. The rule was that we both had to agree completely on the name. Her first name, Faith, came easily. This entire experience from beginning to end was a faith experience with the Lord. I knew in my heart that naming her Faith would be a testimony to others as to what God could do in a life. Her middle name was much more difficult to agree on. We each looked at names, throwing them back and forth. Finally, I brought the name Sariah (pronounced suh-rye-ah) to Michelle. She was sold! She had seen the name in her own search and loved it. It means Princess of the Lord and seemed perfectly fitting for our princess. We named her Faith Sariah Orr.

After getting the call from the birth family, I began to reflect on the promise mentioned above that I received seventeen years earlier while sitting in a university chapel service. I felt the Lord had impressed upon me that day that He would restore everything the locusts of sin had eaten, referring to a passage in the book of Joel. First, God supplied me a wife that I loved very much. We had built a great marriage, and I was grateful for her. Now God had worked miraculously to give me a daughter. Tears flowed freely down my face that evening as the magnitude of the blessing began to grip my heart. God had been faithful to his promise.

The day we called about adopting a child with Down syndrome was May 26, 2009. The day we took her in as our daughter was July 17, 2009. Amazingly, from the time of our phone call with the birth parents until the time we adopted Faith was seven weeks. Not only that, Michelle's assurance that we would have a child by Christmas came to pass. On December 10, 2009, we became a forever family in the eyes of the court. God was working indeed.

Conclusion

This is how our adoption came to be. However, God still had work do in my heart as well as Michelle's. To do this heart work, He would use two of our old friends, Randy and Annette.

Chapter 7

One Final Work

G od's redemptive work preparing us to be Faith's parents was nearly complete by 2008. When we began to attend Kings Point, Randy and Annette, together with their church, were so gracious to us. They ministered to us as a church family and supported us all through our adoption experience. Years earlier, they had adopted their son and had experiences they shared with us through the process. Michelle and I recall the day Randy introduced his son to the congregation, kind of like Simba in *The Lion King*, held high for all to see. Surely God had brought our families together at this time to help us through our own adoption experience.

Dreams of my Father

The purpose for going to Kings Point and rejoining Randy and Annette for that two year period was for more than our shared adoption experience, however. God was dealing with lingering issues regarding my relationship with my father in order to prepare me to be Faith's father.

The transformation process actually started nearly three years before we first attended Kings Point. My grandfather had sent me a letter that shook me to the core. It wasn't uncommon for him to send me the occasional letter, detailing what was happening in his life. When I received the letter that day, I expected to find out how his health was progressing or how grandma was doing, or his take on the national news. However, the normal letter was not to be. Instead, he informed me that a nursing home had contacted him to let him know that my father, his son, was dying of brain cancer. When I heard the news, I couldn't help but think about my relationship with my father over the previous several years. I didn't see him much from the time I was fifteen when he drove away that day at my home to the time I was twenty-two years-old, a year after my conversion. To make sense of what happened during the period, I will need to explain a little background of our relationship.

At the age of twenty-one, I came to know Christ via my introduction to Alcoholics Anonymous (AA). It was there that I learned about the twelve steps that lead people to recovery. Almost immediately, I began to work through those steps with the help of a sponsor. My sponsor encouraged me to make a list of the people I had harmed by my selfish behavior. I sought to make amends to people I had harmed in the past as well as forgive those people who had harmed me.

My dad was on the top of my list. He had physically abused my mom as well as emotionally abused me and my brother. At the age of twenty-two, a full year after my conversion, I received encouragement from fellow A.A. members to visit him and make amends. I finally worked up the gumption to go to him and ask his forgiveness for rejecting him at the age of fifteen. Even though he had hurt me, too, I decided not to bring up my need to forgive him and his sin against me. My intent was to clear my side of the street alone.

A few days later, after deciding to make amends, I drove to my dad's house to talk to him. When I arrived, I knocked on the door. He answered and reluctantly allowed me to come in to his home. He opened the door slowly and asked me what I wanted. I replied that I simply wanted to talk to him. When he let me in, he turned his back and walked toward the couch, sat down, and proceeded to watch television. Not knowing quite what to do, since my dad had made the situation awkward as he oftentimes did, I sat down and told him how I had discovered I was an alcoholic and had joined AA.

I let him know that part of the program consisted of cleaning up my past. I explained that I was sorry if I had done anything to hurt him. I specifically apologized for the time I didn't go to his house when I was fifteen. I knew that this was part of the reason our relationship had been severed.

The whole time I was talking, he never looked at me once but simply continued to gaze intently at the television. After I finished, I told him I had to go. In a voice with a hint of frustration for my interruption of his day, he instructed me to lock the door on my way out. Those were the only words from my father during this interaction, yet, despite his calloused response, I felt that a burden had lifted off my shoulders. What I didn't realize at the time, however, was that God still had work to do.

In the ensuing years, usually during the Christmas holiday, I stopped by and visited him. Sometimes when I attempted to visit him he wasn't interested. When I knocked, he would peek out the window to see who was knocking. When he saw that it was me, he would turn off the lights and go to bed. All I wanted to do was see him once a year, visit him, and tell him that I loved him. I also wanted desperately for him to tell me he loved me and that he was proud of me, something of which he wanted no part.

Then, after I was married a couple years later, my wife joined me for my yearly visits. On a Christmas holiday, a few years after I was married, Michelle and I stopped by one evening, shortly before Christmas. She was a little nervous because we had visited a few times before, having received mixed receptions. Sometimes he would let us in and sometimes he wouldn't. Each time, however, was very painful because, clearly, my dad really didn't care to see me.

Then came the final time I would visit him, and Michelle was with me. When we got out of the car, we slowly walked together up to his door. I knocked a few times but no answer. I knew he was home because the light was on and the television was playing. After a few more knocks, my dad peeked out the window and saw who it was. He angrily asked us to go away. Immediately, he turned off the lights and the TV and went to bed.

Discouraged and hurt, I walked back to the car, with Michelle holding my hand the entire time. When he had rejected me in the past, I was able to brush it off. This time was different. After we got into the car to leave, she spotted the pain on my face, mirroring what was taking place on the inside. She began to cry. After a minute or two, she was able to compose herself and asked me a question, which jolted me into reality.

She asked, "Why do you let him do this to you?"

As soon as she said that, I knew she was right. I stopped visiting him from then on, but my feelings of unforgiveness toward him reemerged, unbeknownst to me at the time. I thought I had already forgiven him and didn't need to forgive him again.

God at Work

Those visits and attempted visits with my dad took place in the early to mid-nineties. Now, a decade later, I was ministering in Bloomfield, IN and had just received that fateful letter from my grandfather about my dad's situation with the nursing home and brain cancer. It was quite a shock to get this news, and we responded immediately.

When I went and visited him at the nursing home, I remember talking to him about how he was doing. At that time, he still hadn't come to grips with the fact that he was dying as he firmly believed he was getting better, not worse. He believed there was a cure around the corner. Unfortunately, the coming weeks would tell a different story as his health slowly turned worse. Finally, in December of that same year he would breathe his last breath and be whisked into eternity.

The night he passed away, I was preparing to participate in a Christmas service at church when suddenly I received a call from my brother. He said my dad had passed away and asked me to come immediately to see him before his body would be taken to the funeral home. On the way there, which was about an hour's drive, I started to reflect on our relationship over the years. The pain that still lingered in my heart surfaced. I realized the relationship that could have been, now would never be. I loved my dad, but till his dying breath, he never told me he loved me. I now knew I would never hear those words.

God continued to minister to me in this area for the next several years. Since I was involved in ministry, tending to other people's problems, I avoided dealing with this issue of my own. God wanted to serve me in His shepherding role, but I wouldn't let Him. What I needed at the time was to pursue God, pour my heart out to Him, and receive God's healing. Instead, I immersed myself in ministry which allowed me to blind myself from the real issue.

Kings Point Experience

Once I resigned the pastorate in Bloomfield toward the end of 2007, we found that we couldn't settle on a church in our city.

As I prayed about our situation, God showed me that Michelle and I were to make Kings Point our new church home, at least for the time being. This is where my mentor, Randy Ballard, served as pastor. Since we lived in Indiana, and the church was in Ohio, almost two hours away, the decision made no sense. In spite of that, the more I prayed about the situation, the more God confirmed in my heart that this was the right move.

I always thought of Randy as a spiritual father just as Michelle always thought of Annette as a spiritual mother. But another connection took place, at least for me. Each Sunday Michelle and I ventured over to Kings Point, had church, went out to eat with Randy and Annette, and then made the two hour journey back home. We were developing a strong connection again with our mentors, the church family, and a newfound connection with Randy's adopted son, Gabe.

Randy started inviting me to attend his son's football games. He was the star kicker.

After the first game, he invited me to the next game. As the season went on, I ended up attending almost all of his games. Something began to happen to me the more I hung out with the family. I was developing feelings of a family bond for that period of time at least. This was something I had never encountered before. My childhood experiences never allowed me to form such an emotional bond with my family. The rekindling of this relationship was a divine work much needed in my life.

Despite what God was doing, at first Michelle did not like the decision to attend Kings Point, but she had good reason.

She was spending four hours every Sunday driving to Ohio and back after working fifty hours a week teaching school. While she was certainly frustrated from time to time about this move, she trusted me. For two years, she and I made the trip every Sunday, not completely knowing why until the end.

Randy and I Reunite

There was a reason why God had to reunite me with one certain person. I met Randy roughly ten months after my conversion. At that time, I was basically a mess. I had just turned twenty-one years old and had burned virtually every relationship bridge in my life due to my selfishness and addictive behavior.

When we first met, Randy was a pastor in his early thirties who had resurrected a declining church. When he arrived, the church averaged twenty to thirty in attendance. When I arrived, the average attendance was nearly 200 people. His success was due to his ability to develop leaders and make disciples, while teaching others to do so as well. I have lived in the church world for several years now and have seen pastors who were good leaders who in turn developed ordinary people into leaders. Randy, on the other hand, had a knack to develop and shepherd people who came from difficult pasts like mine.

When I arrived, to borrow a jewelry analogy, I was a lump of coal, far from anything that resembled a diamond. Nevertheless, Randy saw something in me no one else had. For the first time, I had an adult male who believed in me. My father never did nor my step-father after him. They forfeited the opportunity to teach me to be a husband or a father. This left me with a gaping hole in my heart and an insecurity that hindered me from accomplishing things that I had the talent to accomplish. So it was natural that I would turn to Randy to fulfill this role.

An Issue of the Heart

My heavenly Father had to settle this issue in my heart because it hindered our relationship. This, in turn, would have hindered my effectiveness as a father to Faith. I believe fathers are to model the very heart of God to their children. The Scripture abounds with examples of how God loves people. The often quoted verse from the book of John reads, "For God so loved the world, that He gave His only Son, that whoever believes in Him should not perish but have eternal life" (John 3:16). The first point to notice in this verse is who God loves. It is the world. God doesn't love some and dislike others. He doesn't love the Germans and hate the Arabs. He loves everyone, meaning His love is unconditional. The Greek term for this kind of love is agape, a term that conveys a type of love rooted in a volitional decision. This type of love doesn't establish a set of conditions for loving someone. This love is unconditional.

One way this type of love is illustrated is by the love the father has for his son in the parable of the prodigal son found in Luke 15:11-32. In the story, the father gives the younger son his portion of the inheritance before he dies. Instead of saving it or investing it wisely, he spends it on wasteful living. After receiving his share of his father's estate, he "gathered all he had and took a journey into a far country, and there he squandered his property in reckless living" (Luke 15:13). Such an act would have caused great shame to the family in a first century Jewish culture, reflecting the typical response in an honor/shame culture.

In this culture the social dynamic in which society is organized maintains social order by inflicting shame on those who don't obey the rules with a twin threat of ostracism. If a son did what the younger son did in the story, the father's response would have been to disown him. However, the story is countercultural in that when the son finally came to his senses and returned home, the father welcomed him with open arms. The father ran toward him when he saw the son coming from afar. The father exhibited the same love that the heavenly Father exhibits toward His children.

Given my relationship with my earthly father, my understanding of my heavenly Father was distorted. My creedal understanding of God was thoroughly orthodox. It was my experiential understanding that needed changing. My understanding of God was that of a heavenly tyrant whom I could never please. So it was difficult to have the Father's heart without truly understanding fully the love God had for me. I needed God to change this in a real way. God used a few means to do this.

Encounter Meetings

One of those means was through Encounter meetings, which were essentially men's retreats on steroids. At this point, my theology had shifted toward a Reformed Baptist understanding of Christianity, having rejected key tenants of Pentecostal theology. Nonetheless, I found myself in the middle of a Pentecostal men's retreat seeking God with everything I had. This far more spiritually intense atmosphere refreshed me since it was different than most men's retreats I had attended before. Most of the time is dedicated to seeking God. The weekend began in a more typical way on Friday with an opening service topped off with a nice meal and great fellowship.

The latter part of the first evening we sought God alone by prayer and Scripture reading. Then the next day we woke up early, for me around 6 a.m., for Bible study and prayer. Around 8:00 a.m., shortly after breakfast, the first session began, usually taught by a lay teacher. This session was the first of many throughout the day and evening. The intensity in seeking God set this retreat apart from other men's retreats I had attended in the past.

During the Saturday session, the teaching focused on forgiving people from your past. I was sitting at my seat, listening intently to the speaker, when the Holy Spirit brought to my mind the need to forgive my father. Initially, I hesitated and justified myself by saying I had already forgiven him. The truth was, I hadn't fully forgiven him.

As the teacher finished his lesson, he gave an altar call. Suddenly, the conviction of the Holy Spirit intensified. I found myself weeping at my seat. I responded by answering the altar call and pouring my heart out to God. I told God how much I hated my dad. I never knew how much he had hurt me until that day. After expressing my true feelings, I confessed the sinful attitudes I had toward my father and asked God's forgiveness. I immediately felt a rush of joy which engulfed my heart. The hurt was already beginning to be removed and healing began. I was changed that day. I began to understand in a deeper way how much God loved me.

We understand God's love through the lens of the gospel. The gospel lets me know that I was a sinner and needed God's redemptive work to justify me because I was dead in my sin.

Jesus has paid the ultimate price for my salvation, taking my sin upon Him and, in exchange, I received His free grace by accepting God's gift of salvation. Because I had been completely and totally forgiven for an offense I couldn't pay, I am to likewise forgive the people in my life. The revelation of my sin, together with a fresh illumination of the gospel, helped me forgive my earthly father.

A Life Changed

This service played a part in determining what kind of father I would be. Had this situation not been rectified in my heart, God's plan to have a father's heart modeled after Him would have been difficult. Christian counselors tell us there are ramifications for not having this kind of heart. Without knowing the grace of God more fully, I might have turned into the performance-oriented father who demands, in an unhealthy way, perfection and obedience. Or, conversely, I might have been an absentee father who would have left Faith with abandonment issues, as I threw myself into my work. Instead, my heart was changed, and I had a fresh understanding of His love. My perception of God was shaped by the anger I held against my father. It was still hard for me to forgive someone who had hurt me so deeply. As God opened my eyes to my situation, I happened to listen to a sermon by Chip Ingram in which he talked about having an inaccurate perception of God. He referred to a time several years back when he had read A. W. Tozer's book, *Knowledge of the Holy*, during a similar time in his life. Tozer distinguished between a creedal perception of God and an actual perception of God. My creedal perception was entirely orthodox, completely in line with the historic Christian faith. My real perception needed some tweaking. I never felt like I was fully forgiven so I never felt fully loved by God. This made it difficult for me to forgive. However, as God was doing His work, I came across Ephesians 1:16-18 which reads,

"I do not cease to give thanks for you, remembering you in my prayers, that the God of our Lord Jesus Christ, the Father of glory, may give you the Spirit of wisdom and of revelation in the knowledge of him, having the eyes of your hearts enlightened, that you may know what is the hope to which he has called you, what are the riches of his glorious inheritance in the saints."

Paul's prayer let me know I needed the Holy Spirit to illuminate the truth of these verses, something He did. In verses 3-14 Paul outlines the riches of the gospel. These verses show the need to have the Holy Spirit continue to illuminate these truths to our hearts after we are Christians. That night, when God began to enlighten my heart regarding these truths, I found it much easier to forgive. Since then, I see the continued need to deepen my understanding of the gospel. As I study and meditate on these truths, my love for God also deepens. Now, finally, God had prepared me to be Faith's dad.

Michelle's Encounter

Michelle remembers the day I told her about Encounters at Kings Point Church of God.

Immediately, she had reservations and did not want to go. She thought of many reasons not to attend, but later discovered that this was common for many women because of the spiritual battle that happens at Encounters before, during and even after the events.

Fortunately, Michelle made it to her first Encounter. She found it different than any other women's retreat or event she had ever attended. The prayers going on in preparation brought a presence of the Lord she had not experienced often in her Christian walk.

This Encounter deepened one's relationship with God instead of focusing on fellowship with other women. The first night and following day, each lady did some deep thinking and praying about where they were in their relationship with God and analyzed their personal histories.

For example, Michelle had much pain surrounding some childhood experiences that only God could mend. She was able to lay those things at His feet never to take them up again.

God ministered to her in her identity in Christ. By rehearsing the enemy's lies, she allowed him to continually lie to her. For the first time, she was able to confront those lies with the truth of God, and, while not completely free, she felt victory in this area of her life. Through this incredible experience, she took some time to really seek God, humble herself in prayer with other Christian women, and determine not to let the enemy feed her his lies any longer.

For the last day of Encounter, they celebrated and focused outward to others who were hurting and in need of a Savior. Following the Encounter, the women were sent back to their home churches with the mission to reach others for Christ and not return to the old ways they were living before they came.

One significant session centered on a woman who had difficulty having children and finally became pregnant. Michelle decided to go forward for prayer about her own barrenness. She believed that God intervened supernaturally to do some deep healing in her heart during that session that would help her to become the mom Faith needed.

Not long after that, Michelle and I made strides in adopting our precious daughter. We look back on those experiences with fondness. In many ways God was performing spiritual surgery, preparing us for something great.

I am reminded of the bear that was rambling through the woods minding his own business when, suddenly, he felt the clutch of a bear trap on his ankle. The trap sank deep within his limb resulting in much pain.

Soon a hunter, the one who set the bear trap, saw the bear agonizing in pain. Surprisingly, the hunter had sympathy on the bear and decided to let him go. To do so required the hunter to dislodge the bear's foot which caused the bear much pain. Thankfully the pain was short lived, and necessary to endure for freedom to take place. In a sense, the pain was a needed precursor to freedom.

Likewise, we endured a similar experience. We had to deal with some pain in order for freedom to take place. God took us through the necessary steps to bring us to a place where we could receive one of life's greatest blessings, having a child of our own.

Chapter 8

Preparing to Adopt

While transforming our lives, God was preparing us to adopt. Randy and Annette walked us through the adoption process as they had adopted their son, Gabriel, several years earlier, while we attended their church in Terre Haute. They helped us by sharing advice from their own experience with the joys and possible disappointments of adoption.

The majority of these conversations took place at lunch after church, at one of our three favorite places, b.d.'s Mongolian Grill, Chipotles, and another local Mexican restaurant. There we talked about the service, ministry, and Gabe's football game from the previous Friday evening. We also talked about adoption. They told us about the joy of being parents when they thought they would never be able to experience that joy.

At one point, I asked a very straightforward question. When I did, I noticed my wife glaring at me as soon as I asked it. I just wondered if having an adopted baby really felt like your own.

After all, it was someone else's child by birth. They politely explained to me that the bond that is developed between an adoptive parent and the child is just as strong. They said that they see Gabe as their real son, as if they gave birth to him. This helped a lot.

They also shared that there were times when they thought they were getting a child, and something would come up. The birth mother might change her mind, for example. Knowing these experiences helped to prepare Michelle and me for possible future disappointments. The adoption process is never easy, and there are always disappointments along the way.

As time went on, we continued our adoption conversations. During one of those conversations, Annette encouraged us to pray for the birth mother, both before and after the adoption. Michelle and I hadn't really thought of that. Certainly, the safety of the mother and child is always at the forefront of the Christian adoptive parents' mind before the birth mother has the child. Friends, family, and fellow church members offer daily prayers for a safe birth. What is often forgotten, however, is the need to pray for the birth mother after the adoptive parents assume custody of the child. After carrying the child for nine months, and feeling the emotional bond that a mother feels for her child, there is a process of grief the birth mother goes through. Annette recommended that we pray that God minister to the birth mom and help her deal with any guilt, shame, sadness or depression. Michelle and I prayed together

often for her in particular as well as the birth father and their extended family.

The Church Reached out to Us

Throughout the process, Randy brought our adoption as a prayer request before the church, and they prayed for us regularly. We went through the process together as a biblical community.

The church baby shower demonstrated the congregation's love for Faith. Annette, along with several ladies from the church, planned it. They went above and beyond the call of duty. When Michelle brought home all the gifts, both she and I were overwhelmed by their love and generosity. We did not have to buy clothes for the first few years after Faith was born nor diapers or wipes for the first several months. When I discovered the cost of diapers, I was even more appreciative of what they had done.

The heartfelt messages they wrote about and to Faith were particularly special and further reflected their love for our little girl. Here are some examples:

Hi Sweet Baby Faith!
Welcome! Your church family is so happy to have you here!

May the God of hope fill you with all joy and peace as you trust in Him, so that you may overflow with the hope by the power of the Holy Spirit. We love you!

Faith, I am so glad you have become a part of Tim and Michelle's family. You are a blessing from God and a very special little girl. You will be loved and well taken care of. May God be a light in your life and road in your life. I love you!

You are fearfully and wonderfully made. (Psalms 139:14) God made you the way you are for a reason. He has a great purpose and plan for your life. Remember you are special because He created you and He will always be with you. Love you and God bless!

God has blessed them with you in their lives. You are a blessed gift from God. Our prayers will be with you as you grow and become a lovely young girl, a teen, then finally an adult. Put your trust and faith in Jesus and your life will be blessed. God loves you and so do I!

There were many more notes that I could share that were equally as thoughtful and showed how much each lady loved Faith. Later, as they interacted with Faith, their love far outweighed the notes that were written. This church family blessed us so much.

Faith would have four more baby showers before it was all over. I guess this is what happens when you wait until you are in your forties to have your first child. At our age, you have accumulated many friends over the years who want to celebrate the event with you. We were so grateful for the outpouring of love and support on Faith's behalf.

Chapter 9

Faith Arrives

A Crisis of Faith

As the big day of Faith's arrival approached, Michelle and I were cleared to talk with the doctor and find out Faith's medical status. When we arrived, we assumed that the doctors would go over all of the possible scenarios regarding the health concerns associated with Down syndrome. While they did do that, the doctors also informed us that there was a good chance that Faith might have *Dandy Walker syndrome*. The doctors shared that if this diagnosis were correct, Faith could have a brain malformation where there is a missing part of the brain between the two hemispheres. If true, it meant Faith would likely not walk, talk, or even be able to feed herself. It also meant she may have a shortened life span. Michelle and I were devastated. The thought that there was a possibility that we could lose our child before we even met her weighed heavily on us.

As we traveled home, Michelle sobbed uncontrollably. We had had no idea that this was a possibility. When we finally arrived back at the house, I sat down in front of my computer feverishly researching everything I could find about this syndrome. Michelle, on the other hand, went into the baby's room, prostrated herself with face to the floor, and began to cry out to God. A little while later, she called one of her friends to come over and console her and pray with her.

While Michelle was waiting on her friend to arrive, I decided to call my mom and tell her the news. When she answered the phone, I told her the diagnosis. Her answer hit home. She told me that when I was younger, during one of my stays at Riley Hospital, she remembered a woman who gave birth to a severely deformed young girl. My mom recalls that the girl's mother said, "I can't raise someone like that," so she left and never came back. As soon as my mom told me the story, I knew that I couldn't be that type of parent. God had made it clear to me that Faith was our daughter, and no disease was going to change that fact. Even if it meant raising a daughter with this degree of disability, we would do it.

Once Michelle's friend arrived, they immediately went back to Faith's crib and started to pray. Up to this point Michelle hadn't been able to form words for prayer. Instead, her time was spent in tears and groaning before the Lord. She remembers that her friend prayed that Faith was created in the image of God and that He had her in the palm of His hand. Nothing could touch her without His say so. Finally, Michelle was able to utter words in prayer and shares that she felt almost a literal burden lift from her shoulders. She knew in that moment that either Faith would be completely fine, or God would provide a means of handling any problems that Faith might have. We are so thankful that we made the commitment to our daughter and refused to back out.

Faith is Born

On July 17, 2009, just a few days after the fateful doctor's visit, we received the call that Faith was born. The birth father told my wife that the hospital would transfer Faith after they got her and the birth mother stabilized. We were overjoyed.

Despite our excitement, we still weren't sure what lie ahead regarding Faith's health. We knew, however, that God was in control. On the way to the hospital, which was about 90 minutes away, Michelle and I discussed the many possible health scenarios. However, despite the possibilities, she was our daughter now and we could hardly contain our excitement on that trip to meet her.

Finally, she arrived at the hospital by ambulance after traveling from her birth family's city to Indianapolis. Elated that she had arrived into the world, we still were very concerned about her medical condition. Did she have the Dandy Walker syndrome? Would she ever walk or talk? Would we have to bathe her and feed her for the rest of her life because she would not be able to do it for herself? These questions raced through our minds along with the excitement of meeting her.

Once Faith arrived, they brought her to the Neonatal Intensive Care (NIC) Unit, where the newborns, mostly preemies, were. The room included several baby beds, sectioned off by small walls that divided up small areas for families to visit their babies.

Then we saw her. It seemed like the world just melted away, and if you look at our very first family picture you will see that we instantly fell in love with our precious daughter. One thing we both noticed was that Faith's arms and legs were quite active, a good sign, we thought.

A few doctors came by to check on her within the first couple hours we were there. But the doctor we were waiting to see was the neurologist. When he came by to check on Faith, we immediately wanted his opinion. There was a long line of machines waiting to look at Faith's insides. He looked at the technician working the machine at the front of the line and instructed her to show him Faith's brain. He said to her, "We need to diagnose Faith immediately so we can put her parents' minds to rest." The technician said he would need an order to do that. He immediately walked around the corner, wrote one, and handed it over.

He then performed the test in front of us and said, with a twinkle in his eye, "Your daughter is fine. I see a fully developed cerebellum and no water on the brain." Overcome with a sense of relief, I looked at Michelle as she received the news and noticed the tears of joy flowing down her face. We both had an incredible sense of God's faithfulness and could now fully enjoy the arrival of our beautiful baby girl.

That is how our hospital journey began. We knew beforehand that Faith would be born with duodenal atresia, an ailment that babies with Down syndrome are oftentimes born with. It is an intestinal obstruction that is easily cured with surgery but fatal if left unattended. The two month hospital stay that Faith endured was not a shock, but it tried us in many ways. The journey to healing would take the full two months to complete.

I realized I was now playing the role that my mom played when I was a child. Growing up I had around twenty surgeries, according to mom's count, at Riley Hospital for the first several years of my life repairing my cleft lip, cleft pallet, and deformed hand. During these stays, my mom lived at the hospital, sleeping on couches and eating out of the canteen as I was recovering from surgery. Sometimes the recovery period would take one or two weeks, depending how the surgery went. Nonetheless, she was there. Michelle and I were now the ones sleeping on the couches and eating the tasty microwavable sandwiches, complete with processed meat and cheese as my mom had done several years before.

Faith stayed in the NIC unit the whole time. Most of the babies were premature, weighing just a few pounds. Faith, on the other hand, weighed over eight pounds. I often joked that if the hospital put together a basketball team, Faith would play the center position.

The whole time we were there, we saw so many babies come and go. Some of the babies were there for a day or two while others had been there for weeks or even months. Whenever a baby went home, we had joy for that family, but also a sense of sadness wondering when it would be our turn.

During our stay, we also witnessed heartbreak. In the two months we were there, at least three babies died while on the unit. Each time a baby passed away, we noticed that a song was sung, and the infant was ceremoniously wrapped and taken out the front door later on. Sitting there in the NIC-U, sometimes late at night when this occurred, was very emotional. One evening, a baby passed away just a few beds down from where Faith was sleeping. I could hear the parents lamenting as they lost their little one. While I was listening to what was going on, I looked down at Faith, realizing the precious gift I had been given, thinking how hard it would be to endure losing a child. Our hearts went out to those families. Now that we had a baby of our own, tragedies like these took on a whole new meaning.

Visit our Precious Gift

Over those two months, several friends and family paid visits. The first visitors were my best friend, Jeff, his wife, Melissa, and their daughter, Ariel. Jeff had been my best friend for most of my Christian life, and we knew each other very well. He and I, together with our wives, had served together with the Ballards at their church in Terre Haute several years before. They were like family to us. We were there when Ariel was born several years earlier, and through the years watched Jeff and Melissa raise their daughter into a beautiful young girl. Now, nearly 20 years later, it was our turn, as they were one of the first people to hold our daughter.

My mom and grandmother also visited, which brought back memories of years past.

They, along with my sister and her kids, instantly fell in love with Faith. When they arrived, we were in the lobby area where families could hang out, watch television, and use the hospital computer. Michelle and I spent hours upon hours there. My family each waited their turn as only two people at a time could visit Faith.

My grandmother and my mom were the first to go in. This moment was particularly special for my grandmother, having been in her late 80's at the time she was convinced that this could be the last grandchild she would have before she passed on. She didn't know that my little brother would have a child a few years later for her to enjoy as well. As she made her way to Faith, she couldn't help but voice her excitement. Knowing that Michelle and I couldn't have children of our own, she never thought this day would come. But that day had arrived. As soon as she sat down beside Faith's bed, the nurse gently gathered Faith out of her crib, and nestled her on my grandmother's lap. One could tell by her eyes, my grandmother was smitten by Faith.

She said, "This is the cutest baby I have ever seen." I was pleased by her comment and disappointed at the same time to know that I was now demoted to second place.

My mom had a similar reaction. She relived, at least to some extent, the experience she had several years ago when she gave birth to me, or so she said. She told me that when she had me, she felt impressed that I was special, set apart for a specific purpose. While I don't feel that special calling personally, I do agree about Faith. We all felt that Faith was not only our special gift from God, but that she also impacted many lives for God's glory. Why God chose us to be her parents will be the first question I ask God when I get to heaven. Until then, Michelle and I will joyfully serve as her parents and give her all the love, attention, and training we can in order for her to fulfill everything God has called her to do.

Born to be a Mom

As friend after friend, relative after relative stopped by, everyone echoed the same statement - Faith was special. While this was nice to hear, the way Michelle instantaneously took to motherhood really touched me. Now this did not surprise me in the least, since I had watched her selflessly love and care for countless children over the years as we ministered in various settings. Even so, it brought great joy and satisfaction to see her fulfill a calling God had placed on her life, now in personal motherhood.

As a pastor, I had preached sermons on motherhood and knew of the various scriptures that spoke of motherhood. Now I was able to see it modeled right before my eyes. Michelle selflessly sacrificed as she sat by Faith's bed grabbing an hour of sleep here and there during the night for the first few days. Already, she was the nurturing mother, getting up in the middle of the night when her daughter was sick while listening for every sniffle, knowing just what her child needed.

I also knew of her sincere faith in Christ, which I had witnessed. Her faith would be transferred to Faith as Michelle sought to mold Faith into the person God created her to be.

All of these characteristics and many more are summed up in one chapter from Proverbs. In chapter thirty-one, Solomon revealed the ideal wife and mother. I had seen the description of the Proverbs 31 wife lived out by Michelle, but now I was seeing the Proverbs 31 mother.

Discovered Fatherhood in the Hospital

I often wondered what fatherhood would feel like. For several years on Father's Day, this thought would come flooding to my mind. I didn't much like that day as I didn't have a child or a father to celebrate with. Now things had changed. Faith was my new reason to celebrate.

When I saw Faith for the first time, she was the most adorable little baby I had ever seen.

On the first night, as she lay in her hospital bed sleeping, I felt an incredible sense of gratitude toward God. I was now a father, which felt both great and humbling at the same time. I had studied the concept of fatherhood in the Bible many times before. For years, I sought to draw truths from Scripture to equip men to be good fathers to their children. Suddenly, after having Faith, I knew I had to apply those truths to my own life. From my studies, I knew that I was called to walk in integrity, so I could be a model for Faith to follow (Prov. 20:7). I was not to provoke my child to anger, but teach her the things of God (Eph. 6:4). I was to show compassion to her (Psalm 103:13) and discipline her when necessary (Prov. 13:24). She would be the primary person I was to disciple. What a blessing this was.

Faith is My New Ministry

I had served in ministry for several years before having Faith. I had poured myself out in discipling other Christians serving as their pastor, spending countless hours counseling people, equipping people, building relationships and sharing the gospel. Ministering to broken hearts and broken lives, I fulfilled my calling.

Suddenly, I felt a different calling. Setting aside my aspirations of pastoral ministry, my daughter, Faith, became my new ministry. That ministry started in the hospital the first day I saw her. My feelings of gratitude were tied to my gratitude to God. I had done nothing to deserve this gift. Years before, I was a twenty-one year old alcoholic, contemplating suicide on a daily basis, finding it difficult to function in the daily routine of society without a drink. Now, despite my rebellion, my hatred, and hard heart toward God, He reached down and drew me to Himself. He replaced a heart of stone with one impacted by God's love and grace. Now, with a heart full of gratitude, I was a father.

There is something about the gospel that changes you. While I always knew this, the truth was taking on a special new meaning. Having done a significant work in my heart to prepare me to be a father, the illuminating ministry of the Holy Spirit continued revealing the truth of what I already had in the gospel. The gospel makes clear that before becoming a Christian, I was an unworthy sinner in need of redemption. There was nothing I could have done to save myself. No good work would be enough. No penance would suffice. No human could intercede on my behalf. But Jesus paid the price for my sins by serving as a substitute, taking the penalty of my sin upon Him. He saved me by drawing me to Himself. No work on my part was necessary. I simply accepted the gift. Now, more than ever, the Holy Spirit was crystallizing these truths to me, and I knew that I was deeply loved and fully pleasing to God.

I had an overwhelming sense of how much God's hand continued to orchestrate these events. Loving Michelle and me, He was bestowing on us an incredible gift. The journey to adopt Faith made it abundantly clear God loved us and how blessed we were. He had heard our many prayers. The prayers of a mother who could not have children had been answered as well as the prayers of a father who hated Father's Day because he had no child to celebrate it with. Like Hannah of old, God worked out a miracle and brought a family a child.

The Hospital Stay

The two months we spent in the hospital with Faith were grueling for Michelle and me. After the first week, we drove back and forth every day to spend time with our new daughter. Driving roughly ninety minutes away, we brought our work with us and either did it on the way to see Faith at the hospital or by her side once we arrived.

On the way, we had fast food except on Fridays when we knew we would stay the weekend. The hospital had a special plan for families who had extended stays. They also had a hotel on the campus, and families were allowed two days a week every week. Given the gas prices at the time, coupled with the drive time, we were grateful for the hospital's accommodations. Our weekends, though, were spent living out of a suitcase. As educators and never business people, we found living out of a suitcase every weekend to be a new experience. However, we adapted rather easily.

During Faith's stay at the hospital, we had to learn much to prepare for taking Faith home. For instance, during the first week, the nurse gave me a tutorial on changing a baby's diaper. Since I had to receive training and Michelle didn't, it signaled to me that Michelle was pre-qualified to administer such a duty, but I needed some help. The nurse's intuition was right on target. As she was giving me a tutorial, I felt like this was a waste of time but discovered later that I received some helpful tips. Turns out, it was better to learn the ropes the easy way under a tutor than the hard way by trial and error later.

For the time Faith spent in the hospital, feeding became one of her major issues. She had to have an NG-tube most of the time she spent in the hospital. An NG-tube, also known as a nasogastric tube, is inserted through the nose, past the throat and down to the stomach so children can receive the essential calories and nutrients they would usually receive during normal eating. Because of the NG-tube, it was very difficult for Faith to learn to take the bottle on her own. She never did learn to take the bottle while in the hospital, so it was necessary to put in a G-tube, known as a gastronomy tube. This one is inserted surgically and goes directly to the stomach. The nurses trained us on how to feed her this way, our last hurdle to leave the hospital and take our baby home. It was scary at first, having never done anything like this before. However, once we learned the feeding procedures, we could finally take Faith home!

Once the day arrived, we were overjoyed. As we were packing up her things in the car, we thanked the nurses for all their love and support and bid them farewell. Amazingly, we had accumulated so many gifts and clothes for Faith while at the hospital. Once we had packed up, we were able to take Faith home on her very first car ride. Now Faith was ready to embark on a new journey: life outside the hospital.

Photo Album

Our Wedding Day

Wedding Party

Wedding Traditions

The Nursery is Ready

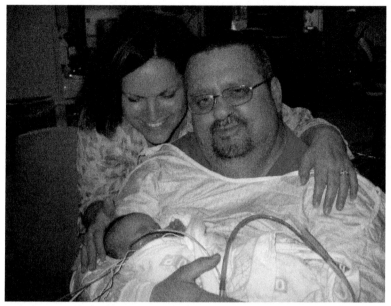

Our First Moments as a Family

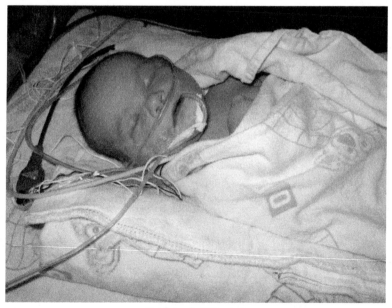

Faith in the Hospital

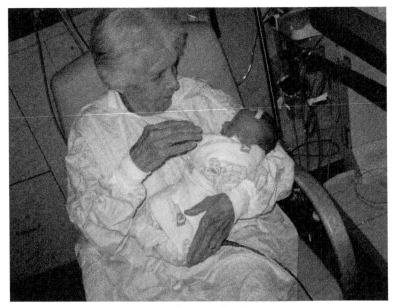

Family Meets Faith

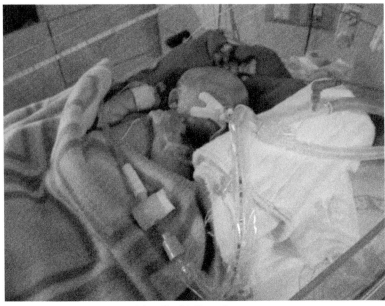

After Faith's First Surgery

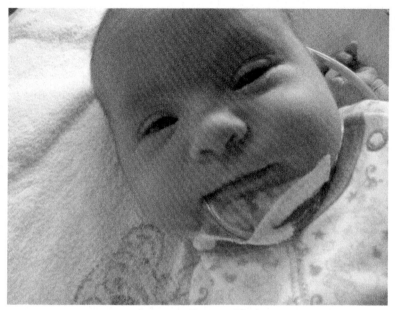

Starting to Become Alert

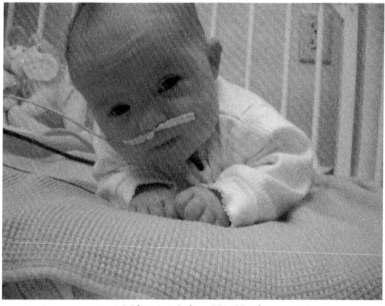

Milestone: Lifting Her Head

Dedication Day With the Ballards

Home at Last!

Empty Bottle

Taking the Bottle

Making Gains

First Sunday School Class

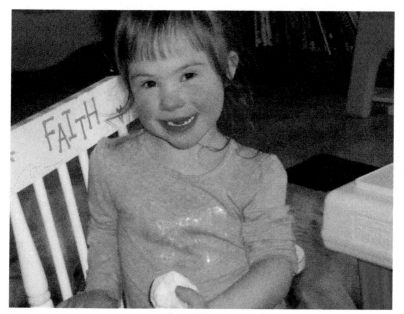

Faith and Her Chair

Faith Loves Her Books

Playing With Friends

Bumble Bee

Faith's Friend, Ishwar

Playing with a Friend

Birthday Sign From Mommy & Daddy

5th Birthday Party

Making Daddy Play-doh Pancakes

Helping Mommy Duke

First Fish! Fishing With Daddy

Mrs. Rogers & Mrs. Bowman, Preschool Teacher & Aide

First Day of Kindergarten

At Grade Level on this Assignment!

Working on Her Name

Note from Faith's Teacher

Reading with Grandma, Michelle's Mom

Hugging Grandma, Tim's Mom

Meeting Grandpa, Michelle's Dad

Michelle with her Grandma

Faith and Daddy

Faith and Mommy

Mother/Daughter Relationship

Christmas Fun!

Growing Up! Looking Forward to the Future

Chapter 10

Making a House a Home

A House versus a Home

Long before Faith was born, Michelle and I always made a distinction between a house and a home. A house, we believed, was simply a physical building comprised of many different features such as walls, ceilings, floors and the like, making up the rooms that comprise the house.

A home, on the other hand, focuses not on things, but people. It is a place where relationships are nurtured and built. People define home in different ways, and Christians have their own perspective of home. While there are certainly disagreements on what all the ingredients should be, there are, I believe, certain essential ingredients that should be in every Christian home. J. R. Miller offers what he believes to be the ideal Christian home.

An ideal Christian home ought to be a place where love rules. It ought to be beautiful, bright, joyous, full of tenderness and affection, a place in which all are growing happier and holier each day. There should never be any discord, any wrangling, any angry words or bitter feelings. The home-life should be a harmonious song without one marring note, day after day. The home, no matter how humble it is, how plain, how small – should be the dearest spot on the earth to each member of the family. It should be made so happy a place, and so full of life, that no matter where one may wander in after years, in any of the ends of the earth – his home should still hold its invisible cords of influence about him, and should ever draw resistless upon his heart. It ought to be the one spot in all the earth, to which he would turn first, when in trouble or in danger. It should be his refuge, in every trial and grief.[4]

Notice, the home is more than just a place to live. It is a place where love, happiness, and harmony rule. It is a place where one finds refuge and not strife after a hard day. A home creates an environment that allows for children to be nurtured

---

[4] Miller, J.R. *Secrets of a Happy Home Life*. Bottom of the Hill Publishing, 2011

in the faith. This is what we want for our daughter. To have a home like this requires both parents present in the rearing of children. In our home, we want to offer Faith a place where she could always be connected with at least one parent at all times.

Jobs and Gender

We had to make some financial decisions. When we decided to adopt Faith, Michelle and I were both working. As an experienced teacher, she made a decent salary. I, on the other hand, had resigned my pastorate a little over a year before and was working as an adjunct professor and substitute teacher.

My theology had changed dramatically, so I felt I could no longer serve as a pastor of a Pentecostal church in good conscience. Employment as a pastor somewhere else was out of the question since I had not yet connected with a different denomination. For us, the decision was not that difficult in terms of who would quit their job. Since my adjunct job was very flexible, I kept that job but surrendered my job as a substitute teacher.

We had to think through how the gender roles would play out. My wife and I are what theologians call complementarian. This means we believe that God has designed men and women in a certain way where they complement one another, justifying the old adage, opposites attract.

The complementarian view assigns the leadership role to the man and the support role to the woman. Ligon Duncan believes "God has created men and women equal in their essential dignity and human personhood, but different and complementary in function with male headship in the home and in the Church."[5] The question Michelle and I had to ask ourselves was, how do we reconcile our complementarian commitments with the occupational situation in which we find ourselves? Traditionally a complementarian relationship consisted of the wife doing all of the housework, while the man worked outside of the home.

As we searched the scriptures together, we found that the Bible really doesn't address much when it comes to the division of labor of gender roles. It does, however, say that women are to give priority to the home. It never says that women should always change the diapers, and men should always change the oil in the car. It also does not say that women should never have to take out the trash, but I digress.

So we didn't see me doing more of the traditional housework as a problem, nor did we see Michelle making more money than me as a problem. Besides, she had always made more money than me. Her job was a source of insurance for us in the ministry, something that is generally pretty costly for churches and ministers, so it was quite a blessing over the years that she could work a job that was family-friendly (no working on weekends or summers) and offered health benefits for the family.

---

[5] Ligon Duncan. "Male Authority and Female Equality: In the beginning— Genesis 1-3 being understood as part of God's created design". *Council on Biblical Manhood and Womanhood*. Retrieved Jan.1, 2015

We needed to work out the idea that the woman has to be the one who stays home with the child during the day. Instead, that role was to be filled by me. Michelle and I worked out a plan in which Michelle could fulfill her duty to give priority to Faith. She fed Faith before she went to work and she would tend to her when she got home. It always seemed that Faith provided the dirtiest diapers during the day while Michelle was at school. I was often the one who got up in the middle of the night if need be so Michelle could be fresh for work, but, to be honest, Faith slept through the night most nights once she got home from the hospital. We approached the child-rearing as a team without surrendering the gender dynamic of father and mother.

Establishing a Father/Daughter Bond

Staying home with Faith allowed me to establish a father and daughter bond that I truly cherish. Not long after we brought her home, I was feeding her one night in our living room, long after Michelle had gone to bed. There was something in Faith's eyes, as far as I was concerned, that said, "This is my daddy." This experience reminded me of a quote I once read from an unknown author that said, "They say that from the instant he lays eyes on her, a father adores his daughter. Whoever she grows up to be, she is always to him that little girl in pigtails. She makes him feel like Christmas. In exchange, he makes a secret promise not to see the awkwardness of her teenage years, the mistakes she makes or the secrets she keeps."[6] The bond transcended any of her future shortcomings, or any of mine for that matter.

God reminded me that night that I had the chance to offer this little girl in my arms something I never could get from my earthly father but did receive from my Heavenly Father. The bond between a father and daughter is something special, and being home with Faith for those first three years helped to establish this bond, ensuring its strength for years to come. As a result of being there to hold her when she was sick or hurting, she learned the safety of a loving father who cared for her. Experiencing a father's love will probably shield her from promiscuity when she gets older.

Sometimes things happen to young girls when they seek out men unscrupulously to fulfill a void left in their hearts from their fathers. My hope is that Faith will never have to do that. Victoria Secunda captures this point quite well when she says,

A daughter needs a loving, available, predict-able father or father figure who can be counted on, whether divorced or at home. She needs his best paternal intentions, even if his efforts occasionally fall short. She needs his maturity and limit setting and sexual oppositeness, so that

---

[6] Simran Khurana, "21 Sweet Father's Day Quotes from Daughters to Dads," About Education, 2015,

*she can function with confidence in the wider
world of adult love and work.*[7]

A Mother's Role

While I was destined to play an important role in Faith's
life, so was Michelle. It was a role that she was tailor-made
to play. Her love for children had always been evident as she
fulfilled that role in the church for years, having served many
little ones over the years. Now she was a mother to one. Faith
had received a very special gift.

Michelle saw motherhood as a women's highest calling and,
for her, it was an incredible blessing to serve in that capacity.
J. R. Miller captures best the picture I see of the woman in my
house who serves as a mother to Faith. He states,

*The woman who makes a sweet, beautiful home,
filling it with love and prayer and purity, is
doing something better than anything else her
hands could find to do beneath the skies. A true
mother is one of the holiest secrets of home
happiness. God sends many beautiful things to
this world, many noble gifts; but no blessing is
richer than that which He bestows in a mother
who has learned love's lessons well, and has*

realized something of the meaning of her sacred calling.[8]

Every day, Michelle shows love for Faith as well her desire to be a godly mother. Though she was working full-time as a teacher, she didn't let the job get in the way of being the mother God had called her to be. Each morning she committed herself to get up a little earlier to read the Bible and pray so she could feed Faith before she went to work. This act spoke volumes to me because Michelle would normally rather sleep in and get up as late as she could than get up earlier; she loves her sleep! Yet, driven by her love for Faith and the burden she felt to connect with her each morning, she was compelled to make this sacrifice.

One humorous moment, at least for me, was when Michelle had already showered, gotten dressed, and was ready for work and proceeded to feed Faith before she planned to leave. I had just walked into the room when Faith, having just been fed, decided to return the favor and offer a large sample of what she just ate on mom's nicely clean blouse. Luckily the day before was laundry day and there were clean wash cloths, towels, and a beautiful blouse waiting to change into. While she didn't see the initial humor in it at the time, we did laugh together about it later that evening.

---

[8] JR Miller, *Secrets of a Happy Home Life* (Bottom of the Hill Publishing, 1894)

After Michelle worked all day, she would come home aroun 4:30 and spend the rest of the evening with Faith, playing with her, feeding her, and bathing her. For the last hours of Faith's day, Michelle was able to give her the time and attention she needed. Michelle worked hard making sure each moment with Faith was precious, and they were.

After Michelle laid Faith down to bed for the night, she would end her day by doing some work to prepare for the next day. She also had a spare hour before she went to bed to spend with me where we either talked or watched television together. Each time I think of the sacrifices she has made, Proverbs 31 comes back to my mind. Two verses in particular, however, stand out that capture Michelle's commitment: "She sets about her work vigorously; her arms are strong for her tasks.She sees that her trading is profitable, and her lamp does not go out at night" (Prov. 31:17-18). Michelle desired to put her family first in the midst of her many responsibilities, much like the woman described in Proverbs.

There is something about a stable home where mom and dad are working together to parent the child that infuses a sense of healthy self-confidence in the child. Knowing that she is deeply loved, she will have the security that this experience brings. When parents affirm the child after she achieves something, whether large or small, it helps to instill a sense of competence. This prepares her for the many challenges she will face in life. It helps her to be a true overcomer.

Chapter 11

She is an Overcomer

Joni Eareckson Tada

Over the years I have heard countless stories about how people have overcome tremendous adversity, but two stories in particular really stand out. The first is Joni Eareckson Tada. She is a quadriplegic best known for her courage to overcome incredible obstacles. In 1967 a diving accident left her a quadriplegic, causing her to spend the rest of her life in a wheelchair. God, however, had big plans for her. Instead of feeling sorry for herself and allowing her medical condition to define what she could and could not do, she refused to let her disability limit her accomplishments.

After her accident, she became an internationally known artist, a gifted singer, and a radio host who reaches tens of thousands of people every day. Her accomplishments don't stop there. She has also written several books and serves as a nationally recognized advocate for disabled persons. Through God's grace, she never let her disability hinder her. She is an overcomer.

Nick Vujicic

A second person who comes to mind is Nick Vujicic. He was born without arms and legs.

Due to these circumstances, he reached such a level of despair that he contemplated suicide. In spite of that, he chose not to stay in this emotional condition. He persevered and refused to be overcome. His parents went a long way in sharing the grace of God, ultimately helping him find true inner transformation. His tenacity, along with his commitment to Christ, has propelled him to become a true example of the grace of God.

These two individuals both refused to give up or allow their circumstances hold them back. They saw limitations as mere temporary obstacles to overcome. Why? Because God was on their side. They were overcomers.

Evidence of an Overcomer

Early on, Michelle and I saw that Faith was this type of overcomer. When we left the hospital to take Faith home for the first time, we were told to expect Faith to need the G-Tube for several months to over a year after she left the hospital. Every day, four or five times a day, we fed Faith through the G-Tube. However, we would always begin with the bottle first so she could train herself to take it. It was amazing how fast she was advancing with drinking out of her bottle. The first week the most she was able to handle was about a fourth of the bottle. Then the week after, she ingested almost a half a bottle. We were so excited. But our excitement was nothing compared to the excitement we felt the following week.

We were finally making the trip to Michigan to visit Michelle's family and celebrate Faith's three month birthday with her final baby shower. When we arrived, Michelle could not wait to introduce Faith to all her family members. About three dozen members showed up, and about half of them, I was meeting for the first time. This was Michelle's first baby, and everyone was so excited for her.

After we ate dinner, I began to feed Faith her bottle. She drank one fourth, then a half, then three fourths of the bottle. Noticing this, Michelle alerted her other family members that this was the first time that Faith had taken so much of the bottle. However, she still wasn't finished. A few minutes later Faith finished the entire bottle. Her accomplishment was met with applause by all. To this day, that bottle is cleaned up and decorated, kept with Faith's baby keepsakes. Michelle will occasionally take out her bottle and explain the story to Faith so she knows her story as well.

This day was the last time she would ever need the G-Tube. While the nurses anticipated that Faith would need this feeding device for many months, possibly even a year or two, she defied the odds. She was able to take her bottle after one short month home from the hospital. Per doctor's recommendation, we kept the Mic-key button, the port that allows feeding, in until the flu season was over, just in case we would need to get fluids in easily, but Faith never took the G-tube for feeding again.

On another occasion, Faith's knack for overcoming obstacles was on display. When she was two years old, I took her for a check-up at the doctor's office. While we were waiting for the nurse to call us in, Faith walked over to the toys where another little girl was playing. The other girl was probably six months younger than Faith, but her physical ability appeared to be more advanced. She sat on the chair with ease as she climbed on it to read a book. The entire time I noticed Faith observing the little girl's every move. Finally, the little girl was called in by the nurse, and her mother gently guided her back to the examination room to see the doctor.

As soon as the little girl left the room, I watched Faith attempt to climb up on the same chair. She tried and tried but to no avail. She simply could not do it. What I didn't know at the time was that Faith was determined to overcome this obstacle no matter what.

Her tenacity continued when we arrived back home and she attempted to climb upon a similar sized chair that our friends had bought for her several months earlier. She tried three or four times to climb on the chair, but again, to no avail. One more time she slipped and fell off the side of the chair leaving her with a slightly bloody lip. I quickly attended to her by cleaning her wound and got her ready for supper. She was obviously frustrated when I asked her to come to the dinner table, as I had interrupted her pursuit to conquer the chair.

At dinner, I told Michelle about Faith's struggle. She showed concern as she expressed sadness for Faith and her experience. After we finished eating, Faith made her way back to the living room. Michelle was a little hesitant to allow her to try to climb on the chair again. However, I persuaded Michelle to let her try one more time. I wanted Faith to discover her own limits and not set those limits for her.

Faith gingerly walked up to the chair, struggled for a few minutes but she finally conquered the chair. Her face told the whole story as she grinned from ear to ear. Michelle and I couldn't contain our excitement. She had conquered the chair This was the first of many times Faith showed such strength in the face of obstacles.

What Faith learned in First Steps

When Faith was still in the hospital, a hospital staff member told us about a government funded program called First Steps. While skeptical at first, I continued to listen and learn more about the program. I discovered that the goal was to provide early intervention to help Faith develop skills to help her in the future. The program connected us with three therapists that served a pivotal role in Faith's physical, motor, and speech development. Each therapist saw Faith for one hour each week and would impact her greatly.

Faith's tenacity to overcome was something I was able to witness as the First Steps therapists visited our home weekly. The first therapist, Lisa, served Faith's physical therapy needs. She focused on Faith's gross motor skills or those skills that involve her mobility including the ability to move around, crawling and walking. Being the parent who stayed home with Faith, I witnessed her grow in her ability to do both of these things. We were told by many health professionals that she would take much longer to develop these skills than someone who didn't have Down syndrome.

According to doctors, Faith would likely not walk before the age of two. Fortunately, no one bothered to tell Faith. After she mastered crawling, she began to work on walking. As new parents Michelle and I so much wanted Faith to crawl and then walk. However, I failed to realize the challenges a child's mobility brings. We had to watch her doubly close, but the trade-off was worth it. She blossomed. Her confidence grew daily as Michelle and I, along with the therapist, worked on her walking skills.

Children with Down syndrome usually have low muscle tone and decreased strength, and Faith was no exception. Yet, her willingness to overcome propelled her development. As any growing child, she wanted to crawl and despite the struggle, failure would not deter her. When her little arms or knees would give out, she simply regained her composure and continued to crawl. When she tried to walk and fell down, she got back up. She would not quit. It simply wasn't in her little vocabulary.

One day, while her physical therapist worked with Faith, the impossible happened. At just under twenty months old Faith took her first steps by herself. It was like seeing a biblical miracle when a once crippled person was able to walk. Faith had overcome another hurdle. She had defied the odds. Not long after, Faith was walking wherever she went.

Denise, Faith's occupational therapist, helped Faith with her fine motor skills, such as dressing, grooming and feeding. Faith really tried hard to master feeding herself. Children with Faith's disability usually have weakened muscles in the cheeks, throat, and tongue which make eating a challenge at first. Again, Faith was not to be denied her victory. With a lot of work and practice, we watched her begin to eat on her own, brush her teeth on her own and dress herself. These qualities are essential now as we get her ready for school each day. Oftentimes, when Michelle and I see her putting her clothes on by herself, brush her teeth by herself, or feed herself, we can't help but think back to those weeks and months where the therapists laid the foundation. Then Michelle and I together helped reinforce and practice what she had learned. As a team, we all helped her develop those skills.

Another important part of the team, the third therapist, worked on Faith's ability to communicate. This skill was essential given Faith's personality type. Early on, we saw her sanguine personality: sociable, energetic, engaged, lively, and carefree. Always moving and on the go, she doesn't slow down unless she is reading a book, one of her great loves. Given

that she loves people, she had to learn to communicate effectively, and her inability to do this would have caused her great
frustration.

Since Faith would be delayed in her speech development, the speech therapist suggested she learn sign language.
Beginning with some basic signs like please, thank you, more,
food, drink, mom, and dad, we could now know when she was
hungry or thirsty, or if she wanted mom or dad.

While her speech began sometime later, she did master one
word early and that was da. Faith would often lie in her bed
saying da over and over and over. Michelle believed that Faith
was just trying to make sounds with her voice, while the word
had no actual meaning to her. She believed this because Faith
hadn't uttered any words sounding like the word mom, but I
digress, again.

Today, her vocabulary is full of many words and phrases
but still is way behind her fellow classmates at school. Even
so, this will not deter her from trying her hardest to learn new
words and means of communication. Faith's unwavering appe-
tite for learning coupled with her desire to overcome drive her
to learn more and more.

She takes a great delight in reading books. Even though
books are very much a part of our home environment, as there
are books everywhere, her desire to read seemed innate, not
necessarily environmental. She was a natural born reader. To
this day, she would rather have someone read a book to her than
watch a television show.

Faith is a Reader

Despite her desire to be a reader, her disability hampered her ability to comprehend the words she was reading. Fortunately, our academic background served to help Faith.

Several years before, I received a graduate degree in elementary education, while Michelle had received one of her Master's degrees that emphasized teaching reading.

Consequently, we were familiar with how children learn by reading. Typically, children's vocabulary grows exponentially if parents read to them early in life. We committed ourselves to spend a minimum of an hour a day reading to our little daughter. Though she didn't understand what we were saying, she was intrigued nonetheless. These early years fostered a love that complemented her God given desire for reading that remains with her today.

As Faith developed her love for reading, she was reading on her own by the age of three. While she didn't understand the words, she mouthed sounds as she pretended to read the books. Her facial expressions told the story as she dramatized what she read. Incredibly, she understood so many things about reading. She knew story, characters, action and plot; she even knew that the letters meant something. Reading in a sing-song voice with lots of emotion, mimicking our reading to her, her emotion went along with the pictures as well.

A little while later, she began reading to her dolls. She would have three or four of them lined up side by side, reading to them the whole time. Faith, obviously, was a natural teacher as she mimicked her parents. Not only did we love to read, we loved to read to Faith. She, then, was extending that same commitment to her dolls. This is one of the blessings of parenthood, seeing your child carry on in your footsteps.

As a parent one has the privilege to develop the next generation by passing on important parenting principles. This was a principle that Solomon, author of the book of Proverbs in the Old Testament, transferred to his children when he said, "Train up a child in the way he should go; even when he is old he will not depart from it" (Prov. 22:6). We hope that Faith will continue her love for learning and never depart from her zeal to overcome.

Conclusion

In those first few years, Michelle and I, along with everyone else who knew her, discovered Faith was born an overcomer. She was willing to battle through adversity, even if it meant conquering the chair and receiving a bloody lip in the process. Not afraid to fail, she strove diligently to learn to crawl then walk. Desiring to be more than a conqueror, she learned to walk several months before anyone thought she could. And, most importantly, she refuses to give up. Faith's natural propensity to overcome made Michelle and me more confident as she started preschool where her limits would be further tested.

Chapter 12

Faith Starts Preschool

◦⸎◦

E very first-time parent dreads their child's first day of school. Traditionally, when the child is born, the parent has five years to prepare themselves as well as their child for this big day.

My first day of school still somehow lingers in my memory. It was the fall of 1975, and Gerald Ford was the President of the United States. He had just become President a year earlier as Richard Nixon resigned the Presidency in shame following the Watergate scandal. My mom was twenty-eight at the time and was ready to send her firstborn son off to school. My brother, who was two years the younger, was able to stay home with mom for two more years before he ventured off to begin his academic career.

A week before school started, my mom went out to buy me new clothes so I could wear them on the first day. As I look back at the pictures now, the clothes I was wearing looked more like clothes that a seventy-year-old would wear on the golf course, not a five-year-old on his first day of school. Back then, plaid pants were in, as well as the bell bottom type pants. On the first day, I was dropped off at the door at Deming Elementary School, and my scholastic career began.

Now, thirty-seven years later, Michelle and I experienced a similar situation as we sent Faith off to her first day of school. Except in this case there was one caveat. She entered school not as a five year-old, but as a three-year-old. Shortly after she was born, we had learned she would start school early; the hospital social worker had helped map Faith's educational future for us. She explained that Faith would spend the first three years receiving physical, occupational, and speech therapy at home through a program called *First Steps*. Once Faith turned three, she would no longer receive those services. The responsibility thereafter would shift to the local school system or private schooling.

Faith Enters the Public School

So, at three-years-old, Faith entered preschool. The school system offered half-day preschool where she received not only instruction but all of her therapies as well. Her placement at Parkside Elementary school seemed to be providential as this was the same school where I had met the little girl whom God used to convince me to adopt a child with Down syndrome those few years earlier.

Faith's daily routine consisted of attending Parkside Elementary School in the morning, then during the afternoon the following year when she was four.

At home, I assumed the honors of getting Faith ready for school each day. Michelle would make sure everything was laid out and ready to go. I drove her to the school where I taught, fulltime, and then the public school bus would come and pick her up about thirty minutes before my school day began. This was one thing I didn't like. It was very difficult for me to put Faith on that bus. It was hard to watch every day because she seemed too young to have to go through that type of daily grind. After her morning at Parkside, Faith was shuttled over by bus back to Columbus Christian School where she and I reunited right before lunch.

To be honest, I wasn't sure at first about the public school system. My hesitancy wasn't motivated by some irrational fear of the "evil" public school system. I hesitated because we had a child with Down syndrome whom we wanted to protect. I had grown up with deformities and knew first-hand how cruel children could be. Michelle and I wanted to protect her from that experience.

We soon discovered that our fears were unfounded. The bus drivers, teachers and staff who took care of Faith's physical, occupational, and language therapy went above and beyond to service Faith's needs. They knew her well and took excellent care of her.

I also discovered that Faith could take care of herself quite well. One day when I came to school to have lunch with Faith, I stood behind her as she went through the lunch line but didn't let her see me. I was about to see Faith in action! This was my opportunity to analyze Faith's social skills. As Faith was going through the line, I noticed the boy next to her trying to take the apple off her plate. It was all I could do not to politely intervene. But I wanted to see how Faith would handle a situation like this one. She was a trooper. Each time the boy reached for the apple, Faith would slap his hand away. He attempted the caper about four or five times, but to no avail. Faith resisted his attempts every time. I was so proud of her. She didn't budge. She refused to be taken advantage of. As I observed, a confidence stirred within me that Faith was going to be just fine. She could take care of herself.

Still, Michelle and I decided that this wasn't enough. Raising Faith for those first three years, we knew her character and strength. The chair experience at the doctor's office clinched it for us. We saw her drive to try and not give up, especially if a same aged peer could do something. Just as she had conquered getting into her chair with ease after practice and effort because another child had done it in front of her, we knew that being around children who didn't have disabilities would challenge Faith to develop faster. We were proven right.

A Star is Born

Another example to me that God would take care of Faith even when we couldn't be there came when I was asked to speak at a local high school on the topic of Down syndrome. I asked if it would be okay if I brought Faith. The teacher leading the class responded with an enthusiastic, "Yes!" I brought Faith to the class with me, and her sanguine personality really began to shine. When she walked in the door, she didn't seem frightened at all. This seemed odd because she was in a place with so many strangers. After I helped remove her coat, she didn't need Daddy anymore; she proceeded to go around the room giving fist bumps to anyone who would reciprocate her request. As I watched in wonder, I saw the students' eyes light up, and saw that, clearly, they had fallen in love with her, too.

Reminiscent of a politician campaigning, Faith's captivating smile engaged the students around the room. The only difference between Faith and a politician, of course, is that Faith's ability to connect is genuine. She genuinely loves people, and people love to be around her.

Parents with disabilities always worry how people will treat their child when he or she is outside of their care. Through God's providential care, He had equipped Faith to take care of herself by giving her a personality and other tools that would help her engage successfully with others.

I also noticed that Faith had a confident stage presence. During my presentation, I told the classes her about her sign language skills. I thought it would be best to demonstrate so

I brought her to front of the class and she took it from there. Normally a child her age would have balked at such a proposition, but not Faith. She confidently taught the class the sign for more, eat, father, mother, grandfather, and grandmother. At the end of the presentation, the kids, thoroughly impressed, gave her a round of applause. Faith had successfully taught her first class. I am not sure who was the most proud, dad or Faith herself.

Christian School Experience

As I have mentioned, peer motivation often drove Faith's learning. She wanted to be able to do what all the other kids could do. Though she received free public school education for half of the day, she would be with children who also had disabilities, many of whom had even more pronounced disabilities than Faith. Therefore, Michelle and I decided that we would use the other half of the day to send her to a private Christian school where she would be in a regular classroom.

Paying for tuition was another matter, however. One day, a friend of ours emailed me about an opening for an elementary school teaching position at Columbus Christian School. This seemed a perfect answer to our dilemma, so I applied. They called me for an interview the following week. Driving over there, I wondered if I could handle teaching as an adjunct professor and be an elementary teacher at the same time. But I was confident that God had opened this door and would supply the energy needed to fulfill all my obligations, which He generously did.

When I arrived for my interview, the secretary greeted me and walked me to the office. As I sat there for a few minutes waiting for the principal and assistant principal to arrive, I was thinking about specific questions they might ask as well as possible questions I would ask them. When they walked in, they welcomed me and began to share about their school. As they did, I got a sense of the genuine care for the students and a real desire to maintain a family-like atmosphere. These two ingredients became an important selling point for me.

Two other perks eventually sold me on taking the position. One was that my room would be right across the hall from Faith's classroom. This meant I could check up on her anytime I wanted. The other perk was that the school gave a fifty percent discount on tuition to all employees. After hearing this, I concluded I would take the job if they were willing to hire me. A few days later, they contacted me and let me know the good news. This began my relationship with Columbus Christian School. On the day I was officially hired, Faith became the latest student to enroll.

We were very pleased with Columbus Christian for several reasons, but one was that this school combined an academic commitment with caring teachers and an incredible sense of community. Michelle and I saw great value in this because in America a sense of community has greatly diminished in recent decades. America used to establish a sense of community centered on families, but now the cohesiveness of the family has been weakened by moral breakdown and divorce (which Michelle and I have witnessed in our own families). Additionally, geographic factors such as family members moving away for better jobs, and a sense of disconnectedness as America becomes more and more individualistic in its pursuits have all managed to strengthen this void.

Consequently, Michelle and I are among many who seek out institutions that cultivate and maintain a sense of community. Many people of my generation or the generations before me most likely remember growing up with this sense of community. Back then, people took care of each other and knew each other. When we first visited Columbus Christian School, we saw immediately that they had established the sense of community that we longed for our daughter to experience. The Columbus Christian community certainly embodied the Latin definition of the word community: *communita*, "things held in common."

Faith's First Day of Preschool

My first day on the job was also be the first day of school for Faith. Little did I know that Faith was about to gain celebrity status. As she walked the halls of the school, her charismatic personality shone bright and caught everyone's attention. After the first few weeks of school, I observed Faith's class walking down the hallway and it seemed that almost every student she walked past knew her by name. This was surprising since she never went out to recess with the older students. Nonetheless, despite limited interaction, her sanguine personality connected on some level, and students of all ages absolutely loved her.

Working at the same school as my daughter provided for some interesting multitasking opportunities. Since Faith only attended Columbus Christian for half of the day, she arrived at school just before lunch. When the bus dropped her off, either Lori or Tammy, the school secretaries, went out to get her and brought her to my room. Faith's response upon arrival was always the same. She would first slap high fives to several of the students before running to me and yelling out, "DADDY!" This was always a great way to end the first part of my day.

I had the Pack n'Play in the back of the room that housed Faith for the last fifteen minutes or so before lunch period began. The last few minutes of class were always difficult as she wanted my attention. Of course, all of this was worth it. We were so appreciative of the school for being family friendly. Allowing us to take those few minutes meant that Michelle and I didn't have to worry about our three-year-old daughter as she went to school. She was under my care and watchful eye as she transitioned to her afternoon class, just across the hallway.

Each day before sending Faith to class, she and I had lunch, and each day this was a blessing. We sat together at my back table where we played and talked. I really loved this bonding time. These occasions cemented our relationship. While Faith may forget having lunch with daddy at three-years-old, I most definitely never will.

As for my students, they absolutely adored her. My girls loved to play with her, fixing her hair, and my boys loved to play catch as two or three of them would gather in a circle with her, tossing the ball back and forth. She had so much fun. At the end of the school day, roughly five minutes after dismissal, my car riding students, smitten by Faith, fought over who got the privilege of gathering Faith from across the hall. After a while, I wised up and had them take turns. Later, I even used it as a behavior modification tool. If they misbehaved, they weren't allowed to go get Faith. Behavior improved immensely, especially toward the end of the day!

There were two teachers who served special roles in Faith's life. If there were ever two teachers who lived out the adage that teaching is a calling, it would be Faith's teacher Mrs. Rogers and her assistant Mrs. Bowman. Their passion for teaching children and their subjects was evident each and every school day. Above all, they had a great understanding of the role they played in the children's lives. They believed that not only were they to develop the kids intellectually but spiritually as well. Our family greatly benefitted from their dedication and love for Faith.

Faith's First Boyfriend

I was surprised to discover that Faith had found her first boyfriend before kindergarten. I never thought this would happen so early in life, especially as early as preschool. I must admit that I am a traditional, protective father. If I could get away with it, I would not let Faith date until she is twenty-five and not marry until she turns thirty. However, she may have other plans, as I soon began to discover.

We noticed that Faith only seemed to know the name of one of her classmates, at least there was only one name she uttered at home. His name was Ishwar. He was from a Sikh family and attended Columbus Christian School. He instantly became Faith's new best friend. I am not sure whether he really became Faith's first official boyfriend, but she definitely seemed to be smitten. When Faith came home from school, though still not able to say many words, one of the words she would say when asked about her day was Ishwar. It was Ishwar this and Ishwar that. Her affection for her friend was clear.

Ishwar's mom, Aman, played an important role in helping to form this relationship. Never seeing Faith as different from the other students, she instead noticed Faith's intelligence and often told Faith's teachers so. Aman transferred this attitude to Ishwar. When Faith had just begun preschool, many of the kids saw her as being different. She wasn't on the same level intellectually as she didn't know many words nor did she talk much at first. Faith largely played by herself, with one exception: she and Ishwar would play like "two peas in a pod" as they say. I believe that since Aman never saw Faith as different, neither did Ishwar.

Now Ishwar, a handsome young man, took a liking to Faith as well. I became privy to this when we invited Ishwar to her fourth birthday party. We had invited several guests and our house was packed with people. Michelle, gifted in children's ministry, had put together several games and activities for the kids to enjoy. Michelle's mom had come to stay a few days and helped with putting together great snacks. Everything was going well. Then there was a knock at the door. Michelle walked over, with Faith trailing behind her. It was Ishwar, his dad, Parminder, and his mom, Aman. As soon as they entered, Faith and Ishwar looked at each other with a look Michelle says she will never forget, a look of tenderness and true love. They reached out and embraced in a friendly hug. Her best friend had arrived, the icing on the cake of an already great birthday party.

We loved watching them interact. As they played the games Michelle was leading, together with Faith's other friends, I noticed that they seemed to be standing next to one another quite a bit. When one of them would do well, the other one would clap, and vice versa. This could be the beginnings of a lifelong friendship. If not, Ishwar will always be Faith's first best friend, and maybe her first love.

Chapter 13

Mother/Daughter Relationship

The relationship between a father and daughter is indeed special, but the relationship between a mother and daughter is equally important. In this relationship, the daughter learns how to be a woman. The mother teaches her to don the many hats she will wear in the future. For instance, a mother will teach her daughter how to relate to the opposite sex by modeling modesty. She will learn motherhood by watching her mother model self-sacrifice as mom tends to the needs of her family. The daughter will learn how to relate with her husband as she observes how mom loves her father. The lessons learned here will allow the daughter to carry these lessons in the future, implementing them in her own family when she begins one later on.

A Committed Mom and Wife

Michelle has always been committed to her family and to becoming the woman that God has called her to be. I have witnessed her love and devotion for almost twenty-two years now and know her commitment to being this kind of woman. I saw her willingness to sacrifice as she followed me to East Chicago to plant a church. Not only did she move there with me, but became my partner in ministry. She saw herself as a helpmate to me. Many women would have never made the sacrifices that Michelle has made for me in ministry. When I felt God call me to pastor a small church in Bloomfield, Indiana, she willingly resigned her job and followed me there. God has rewarded her faithfulness. Each time she quit her job for ministry, God gave her a better paying job in better circumstances.

She has carried over the same commitment to Faith, which has resulted in a special bond. Michelle, the committed mother she is, was the traditional stay-at-home mom the second half of the day as soon as she arrived home from work. Her job, as she saw it, was to care for Faith. In order to allow her the opportunity to do this, I often fixed supper while Michelle was busy reviewing what Faith had learned earlier that day. She would bring her book bag home with papers from both Parkside Elementary where Faith spent part of her day, and Columbus Christian where she spent the other part of the day. Usually it would be a tracing activity or something similar, and Michelle would faithfully make a similar letter and have Faith relearn the letter. Repetition is so important with Faith's disability, something of which Michelle was well aware as a lifelong teacher.

Developed Relationship with Faith

While Michelle's teaching role is important, she also developed a deep relational bond with Faith. There is one role the mother plays that doesn't end when the child leaves the home, and that is the role of confidant. Over the years I have talked to many women who didn't enjoy an enriching mother/daughter relationship. Their experience was characterized by indifference or a judgmental spirit. Conversely, Michelle wanted to have a relationship with Faith that would only grow and blossom into something special as the years went by. During this important developmental stage, Michelle and Faith spent a lot of quality time together.

Mother/Daughter Routines

Knowing the importance of loving routines, Michelle used these to establish her relationship with Faith. These mother/daughter routines exceeded chores to check off the list. The purpose, as Michelle saw it, was not only functional, but also relational. Michelle took activities like bathing, teeth brushing, dressing, and grooming and made them fun so both of them could enjoy doing the routines together. For example, when Faith takes a bath, she goes and gets her own towel and washcloth, goes to the bathroom, and prepares to get into the tub, with Michelle's assistance. Before any serious bathing is done,

Michelle allots about fifteen minutes or so to give Faith an opportunity to play in the water. As Faith plays, Michelle sits next to the bathtub and interacts with her nearly the entire time. When finished, Michelle dries Faith and lets her put on her towel. At the end of the towel, one of the corners is sewed together allowing Faith to put it on her head, with the remaining part of the towel flowing out like a cape. Faith, then, runs back to her room like a super hero. This is one of the highlights of her day. As a result, taking a bath for Faith is also a fun time she gets to relate with Mommy.

Like Mother Like Daughter

Michelle also routinely allows her daughter to be just like her. When Faith sees her mom put up her hair in a band, she wants to do the same. Michelle has learned to have an extra set of bands for Faith so she can join in the fun of being like mommy.

Recently Faith has noticed that Michelle is putting on make-up. Faith learned that word right away. While Michelle is going through putting on the make-up, Faith is sitting right beside her mom learning, as dad likes to call it, the art of face painting. Michelle pretends to put make-up on Faith just like mommy. Faith's face lights up as she engages in this mommy-daughter activity

These times of bonding are valuable lessons. She is learning that her mom loves her and that she is important enough for mom to spend time with her. Furthermore, she is learning that there are differences between men and women, which are values that are in stark conflict with the culture in which she will grow up. After all, daddy doesn't put on makeup, not that it wouldn't help; it certainly couldn't hurt. There are some things only mommies can do for their girls!

Time to Clean Things Up

Third, Michelle has a cleanup routine. She sings a song with Faith right before they begin cleaning up the toys. Faith loves this game, as she sings together with the song. She is usually busy playing with her toys, talking to her dolls or even reading to them when the song begins. Instantly, Faith knows what to do. She is going to clean up her room with mommy's help. As she is doing this, she not only learns the value of personal organization and responsibility, she also discovers the value of a shared activity with mom.

This is a shared activity that won't continue throughout Faith's childhood to be sure.

Soon Faith will only need to be told to clean her room, and that will be the only prompting she will need at least until she becomes a teenager. Nonetheless, a good habit has been established in her life, and that habit also served to strengthen a relationship. Faith may not remember, in total, these experiences, but she will probably remember that Michelle loved her enough to spend that time with her. As a working mother, who works hard every day and is tired when she gets home, Michelle resists the temptation to simply clean up the room after Faith goes to bed. This would have been much easier and far less time consuming but wouldn't have served the all-important relational purpose.

Interesting Stuff

Fourth, Michelle participates in activities alongside Faith. One of Faith's favorite activities is playing with *Play-Doh*. You might remember playing with *Play-Doh* when you were a kid. I do! My grandmother used to come alongside me and make things. One of the things we would make together was log cabins. Those were fun times. Similarly, Faith likes to make things with *Play-Doh*. She seems to want to not only express herself verbally, but creatively through art as well. Michelle has similar qualities. Michelle can make an amazing *Play-Doh* cake or pizza and Faith loves it and copies her the best she can. This shared interest helps to foster a joyful relationship.

You are Doing a Good Job

Lastly, and probably most importantly, Michelle tells Faith how much she loves her and reinforces the good things she does with verbal affirmations. This was something she learned from her grandmother. While I only knew Michelle's grandmother for a short time, as she died about a year or two after we were married, she left an obvious legacy. She was Michelle's biggest fan. The late Howard Hendricks was famous for saying that everyone needs these three relationships in their life if they hope to fulfill the Christian discipleship mandate. They need a

Paul who pours into and mentors them, a Timothy with whom they are sharing their lives by mentoring someone else, and a Barnabas, who is an encourager.[9] For Michelle, her grandmother was her encourager. I see this same Barnabas ministry in Michelle's relationship with Faith.

This last point is played out in a many ways. Michelle routinely affirms Faith when she does something right. For instance, when sets the table correctly, Michelle acknowledges it.

When Faith accomplishes something, Michelle affirms her. As I stated previously, many women grew up only hearing from their mothers what they were doing wrong. For Faith, this won't be the case. Granted, we will correct and point out when she is doing wrong, even offering correction if necessary, but that won't be the only truth that will be spoken. Faith will know that she does well and is loved by her family.

For example, some children grow up getting punished for bad grades but are never rewarded or verbally affirmed for getting good ones. In the book of Ephesians, Paul corrects the father for presumably only punishing but failing to affirm his child. He states, "... do not provoke your children to anger, but bring them up in the discipline and instruction of the Lord" (Eph. 6:4).

Children need to hear their parents affirm them, not in a narcissistic, therapeutic way where the parents inadvertently establish a fragile ego within the child as the child has to receive

---

[9] I heard this quote in a sermon by Chuck Swindoll years ago.

praise to feel secure but reasonable affirmation that builds the child's confidence and instills a feeling of competence. For instance, when the child makes something and brings it home from school, they are complimented for a job well done. If they have done their best, they should be affirmed. Over the years, we have seen Faith develop a feeling of competence, essential for her to overcome obstacles, and her mother certainly played a role in her success through her consistent affirmations.

A child also requires a parent to listen and give him/her physical affection. In essence, Michelle shepherds Faith's heart just as Paul Tripp instructs parents to do in his book, *Shepherding a Child's Heart*. Michelle is pointing Faith to the goodness of God's ways. God does the same for His children. Sometimes Michelle will be grading papers and Faith will be snuggled up next to her playing on her iPad without a care in the world. What this says to Faith is that she is important. She is not left to entertain herself all the time because mom is too tired to spend time with her. Instead, she is welcome and belongs right at mom's side.

Conclusion

Faith and Michelle bond through these times together, making their mother/daughter connection one that will last throughout the years. Laura Ramirez says, "The love between a mother and her daughter is special. A mother takes her daughter under her wing and teaches her how to be a woman. In order to do this, you have to ask yourself what it means to be a woman of today. How do you balance care for others with your own quest for meaning and joy in life and how do you pass on these lessons to your daughter?"[10] Michelle has fulfilled this ideal by looking to the scriptures and applying them to fulfill her calling as a mother. With this firm foundation, I look forward with delight to Faith's future. I pray she will live out God's plan for her life, following her mother's godly example. I look forward to watching her discover and fulfill that plan.

---

[10] http://listverse.com/2012/05/07/top-10-famous-mothers-and-their-daughters/ retrieved on March 9, 2015

Chapter 14

Discovering Terrace Lake

A ll of us have to make critical decisions in life but some of our choices have more lasting consequences than others. One of the most important decisions you and I will make as Christians is membership in a local church. This decision will go a long way to shape your spiritual life and the spiritual life of your family. In the end, church is where you will be challenged and encouraged to live out the Christian faith. Your children will make friends with other children and youth there who hopefully have biblical values. These relationships have the potential to be a source of real blessing.

As a family, we strive to live out our faith as authentically as possible. We want to shine the light of the gospel to the world around us. To do so means we needed a church that would help us continue to grow into a gospel-centered family. In February, 2010, we left Kings Point Church of God and looked for a home church to attend in Columbus, Indiana where we lived.

Six months before, Randy suggested we consider finding a church closer to home. After much prayer, Michelle and I sought out different churches to attend to see which one would be a good fit for us.

As we began our search, we knew the church we were looking for could be our home church for years to come. Consequently, Faith may spend the better part of her childhood there. Because of this we didn't take the decision lightly.

To begin, Michelle and I had to narrow down our priorities. Oftentimes, a family's top priority is whether one's kids like the youth group or children's ministry. While important, we decided this wouldn't be our top priority. We believe that spiritually fit parents raise spiritually fit children.

Through the years, I have witnessed people attending a church for the wrong reasons, and their family pays the price in the long run. A few years ago, a family left our church to attend somewhere else. This is not uncommon and not necessarily wrong all of the time. However, this particular couple told me that they left because their child liked the youth group better at another church. I inquired further and discovered that the ministry was very personality driven. As we continued the conversation, a statement made by the mother struck me. She said she really missed the strong teaching and dynamic worship at the church where I served as an elder. After chit-chatting for a few more minutes, the couple lowered their masks to reveal their troubled hearts. While their children were happy, their marriage was in trouble. My heart went out to them, but I couldn't help but remember why they had left. They had fallen prey to a consumer motivation rather than a biblical one. Now they were reaping the consequences of an ill-advised move.

Our Priority List

There were three things on our personal priority list. The church needed (1) to be committed to the scriptures and sound in theology while instructing the congregation on how to embrace biblical and theological truths, (2) a solid biblical elder team, and (3) to be a place where we could use our spiritual gifts to edify the church. We knew that we could not live as a gospel-centered family without the proper spiritual nurturing that comes with a healthy church relationship.

As part our church search, we attended a couple of the larger churches in the area, but none seemed like a good fit. I then expanded my search to include the two Southern Baptist churches in the area. If I chose the Southern Baptist route, I wanted to attend a non-traditional church of that denomination. In searching the Internet, I discovered there were two strong SBC churches, one traditional and one contemporary. We opted to try the contemporary one, Terrace Lake Community Church.

Committed to Scripture and Sound Theology

In perusing their website, I found that the senior pastor had graduated from Dallas Theological Seminary. This was a real selling point for me because the school is known for producing strong, solid, biblically based Bible teachers. I took this as a signal that the church valued the Bible and theology. My assumptions were later confirmed.

On a cold February morning, Michelle and I bundled up Faith in a coat and blanket and set off to try out Terrace Lake Community Church. At first, the church came across a little seeker sensitive because of the dim lighting during worship and the bright lights on the stage. The term "seeker sensitive" meant the service was designed to meet the "seeker" or non-Christian. I had assumed that the lighting reflected this belief system. Upon further investigation and discussion, the pastor assured me that the church rejected this type of church strategy. The lighting's design is meant to enhance worship, and is not necessarily meant to appeal to a certain demographic.

Clearly, the church had a strong teaching ministry. The exposition of the scripture seemed to be solid, worship was good, and the people were friendly. After the service I wasn't sure if this was going to be our home church, but wanted to give it a try once more. At the time, the church had a Thursday night service once a month, so we again bundled up Faith and off we went.

When we arrived, a few people greeted us at the door, then we walked over to the fellowship hall to the midweek dinner and Bible sharing event. We sat down at one of the tables as the people began to file in. We were a little nervous, but everyone seemed so friendly which eased our fears. At the time, the church was much smaller than it is now, so we interacted with most of the people that were there, at least at some level.

Before the group went in to the sanctuary to discuss the Bible, they ate a meal together.

Michelle and I enjoyed this because it felt like a real community. About halfway through the meal, the pastor came over and talked with me. I told him a little about my background, occupation, and love for apologetics. He echoed my interest and said he loved apologetics also. As we finished our conversation, I surmised that the church seemed to have a strong biblical and intellectual commitment which was important to me.

A Strong Elder Team

I had to do more detective work before I decided. I wanted to be assured the church had a strong elder team. The term elder, synonymous with the term shepherd, features a part of God's revealed nature. God as shepherd connotes God's care for his people, reflected in David's statement, "The Lord is my shepherd, I shall not want" (Psalm 23:1). The people whom God chooses to lead the church are to exhibit this same characteristic in their lives. Thus, elders serve as God's under-shepherds, responsible for the growth, nurture, and care of the local congregation. They must know, feed, lead, and protect the sheep.

I began attending an Adult Bible Fellowship (ABF) class, what most people call a Sunday school class. Two of the elders attended the class, which made for an excellent opportunity to get to know them. I wanted to know if the elders were truly shepherds or more like corporate executives. Did the elders take the Bible seriously? Were they well-versed in the Scriptures?

After sitting in the class for several weeks and interacting with other elders, I was confident the church had a solid elder team, as I saw the qualities of eldership lived out.

Getting Involved

To get involved required we attend the Discovering Terrace Lake class, which was geared toward introducing new people to the church and also served as the prerequisite for membership. Michelle and I attended with great anticipation. The meeting took place at one of the member's homes, located in a nearby subdivision. Six couples attended, along with the staff of the church.

During one of the meetings, the pastor asked me if I would be interested in planting a church. He even said he would be willing to give up fifty people who were interested to help plant it. I discerned that I was in the right place. Though it never materialized, the offer attracted me to come aboard.

I believed I had chosen the right place. A few months later, I felt even more confident in the choice when I was asked to preach on Sunday morning. God gifted me to preach, and I couldn't imagine not being able to use that gift to edify my church family. I preached several times after that. I later led the mission team, taught Bible classes and eventually became an elder.

Michelle also became involved and initiated a new Sunday morning children's ministry a couple of years after we arrived. The ministry has grown much even after she gave up the reigns to someone else, and it still thrives today. Michelle also used her gifts on the worship team, ladies ministry, and by serving alongside me.

I say all of this to show that we're involved in a healthy church where everyone uses their gifts. This is important because healthy churches help build healthy families. Consequently, we have been enriched by our experience there.

Ministry to Faith

The same three commitments that governed the church, filtered down to the children's ministry. Faith has grown up in this church for almost her entire life. As a result, she has received sound teaching from a loving, competent children's staff, as well as care and nurture from them. As the church continues to grow in these areas, she will be nurtured in the faith as she grows older, allowing her to use her gifts to glorify God as a result.

Chapter 15

Nurturing Faith's Spiritual Life

Throughout the time I was an ordained minister, I had to offer advice to parents about parenting. Over the years, I have read quite a bit of material on this subject because I wanted to offer solid advice. But many centuries ago when Solomon penned the book of Proverbs, he gave the most important advice: "Train up a child in the way he should go; even when he is old he will not depart from it" (Prov. 22:6). Thus, a parent's guidance plays a pivotal role in determining the spiritual future of the child.

Michelle and I have tried very hard to offer Faith all the advantages we could give her regarding education, training, and nurturing. However, one responsibility remains most important. If the parent doesn't nurture the spiritual life of the child, then the parent has failed his or her primary responsibility. We are to help Faith with an understanding of the gospel so that she develops a relationship with God. Then we are to continue to nurture that relationship once she comes to Christ. To do this requires that we have a plan for her spiritual life.

Spiritual Development Must Involve Both Parents

As Michelle and I began to map out a parenting strategy, neither one of us wanted to succumb to the idea that the spiritual nurture of the child fell only on the mother. I see this error all too often. Many men have given up their duty to lead their families spiritually. Spiritual nurturing is just as much the father's role as the mother's and should have that additional layer of spiritual leadership.

Historically, men have had an easier time fulfilling their role as spiritual leader. In the past, his role as husband and father in an agrarian society required him to fulfill the responsibility as the home's spiritual leader while spending much time in and around the home. Then came the Industrial Revolution which changed the economic framework of society, and men left home to work in the factory (1780-1830). The primary responsibility of man operating as husband and the father shifted from the man putting his family first to putting his job and career first. This was a different way to take care of the home, and deceived men into thinking they took care of their families in a new way. In essence, they traded home life for another more individualistic kind of life.

This new revolution was based upon the economic philosophy of capitalism. According to Nancy Pearsey, "The [new] capitalist seemed to require each man to function as an individual in competition with other individuals. In this new context, it was appropriate, even necessary, to act under the impulse of self-interest and personal ambition."[11] Now, to simplify things, the wife served the home while the husband went out to work. The role of sole spiritual leader transferred to the wife, releasing the husband from the role of moral and spiritual leader. Men, now free to explore individual pursuits with the goal of providing economically for the family, transitioned into this way of life at the cost of their spiritual health and well-being.[12]

I see it as my job to be the spiritual leader and lovingly serve Michelle and Faith. I am to model the Christian faith to my family and take the initiative to cultivate a Christian atmosphere in my home where prayer and Bible reading abound. Prayerfully, I must construct a parental strategy that honors God.

Two gentlemen greatly informed my understanding of parenting. I read Tedd Trip's book, *Shepherding a Child's Heart* which supplied me with a philosophy of parenting. I also discovered the work of his brother, Paul Tripp, someone who I came to respect for his views on counseling. They both had wise advice and strategies. They had resisted the temptation to integrate secular sources into their parenting and counseling philosophies, while at the same time avoiding the fundamentalism that sometimes characterizes religious-oriented parenting.

---

[11] Nancy Pearsey. *Total Truth: Liberating Christianity from its Cultural Captivity.* (Wheaton, IL: Crossway, 2008)

[12] Ibid.

Instead, they offered a reasoned, well thought through view of parenting, while remaining faithful to Scripture.

Children are Sinful like Their Parents

Early on in this book, I shared about my life before I became a Christian. Obviously, I lived a very sinful lifestyle. My sinful lifestyle stemmed from my fallen nature. What about Faith? Does she have a fallen nature?

The Apostle Paul aptly described mankind's fallen nature when he said, "They are darkened in their understanding, alienated from the life of God because of the ignorance that is in them, due to their hardness of heart" (Eph. 4:18). This alienation, ignorance, and hardness have separated men and women from a relationship with God. Yet, even when redeemed, the sinful nature remains. This sinful predicament encumbers us until we enter into heaven. Even the Apostle Paul admitted his own struggle with sin, a fact he acknowledged in his letter to the Romans (7:17-20). He declared,

> *So now it is no longer I who do it, but sin that dwells within me. For I know that nothing good dwells in me, that is, in my flesh. For I have the desire to do what is right, but not the ability to carry it out. For I do not do the good I want, but the evil I do not want is what I keep on doing. Now if I do what I do not want, it is no longer I who do it, but sin that dwells within me.*

211

If the great Apostle Paul struggled with sin and was handicapped by it, how much more are we who are not one of our Lord's apostles? The sinful nature of men and women is an empirical fact, impossible to deny.

Faith, our beautiful young girl, just five years old, brings delight to our lives. Everybody who knows her, comments on her manners and behavior. Despite this fact, they fail to see the occasional temper tantrums where she demands her own way. They also are shielded from her demands to eat ice cream instead of green beans, or to opt for bananas instead of carrots. Her actions reveal her sinful nature, one that wants to do what she wants to do, despite the suggestion of her mom and dad. Actually, everyone who is born has this same nature, one that drives us to do what we want to do. Ted Tripp was exactly right when he said, "Even a child in the womb and coming from the womb is wayward and sinful. We often are taught that man becomes a sinner when he sins. The Bible teaches that man sins because he is a sinner. Your children are never morally neutral, not even from the womb".[13] The child who is yet to be born, as innocent as he or she would seem, is still hampered with the sin nature inherited from Adam. I surmised that parenting must start with this foundational perspective.

---

[13] Tedd Tripp, *Shepherding a Child's Heart*, (Wapwallopen, PA: Shepherd Press, 1995) 37

Parenting Starts with the Heart

Moralism does not remedy our fallen nature, however tempting it may seem. Instead, it reduces the gospel to nothing more than moral self-improvement. Seducing people to believe that we earn God's approval by our good behavior teaches children that they must be good boys and girls in order to be acceptable. The focus of child-rearing for the moralist is to raise their children "right", whatever that term means. I believe that God has something better to offer parents who want to raise children who have a heart that follows after God.

To decide on a plan to nurture Faith's spiritual life, we began by asking an important question. What is the primary issue to be addressed in the child? The knee-jerk reaction seems obvious: correcting bad behavior and nurturing good behavior. While this is part of the duty of a parent, we didn't think that it was the primary duty.

For us, the core concern of the parent is not the behavior of the child, but the heart of the child. For example, Proverbs 4:23 declares "Keep your heart with all vigilance, for from it flow the springs of life." Solomon knew that one's character or lack thereof, began not by one's actions, but within one's heart. When we apply this scripture to parenting, the primary concern of the parent should be the child's heart. The actions and behavior are like symptoms indicating a problem. Treating the symptoms does not offer a solution. One must go to the source of the problem and eradicate any sinful patterns found in the heart.

The alternative, of course, is behavior modification. Behavior modification can have some outward benefit but doesn't really deal with the sin nature found in the heart. Jesus pointed out that what we say with our mouth begins in the heart when He said, "For out of the abundance of the heart the mouth speaks" (Matt. 12:34b). Jesus was responding to the Pharisees who acted religiously in their behavior without addressing the heart.

Elsewhere, Jesus rebuked the Pharisees when He declared, "Woe to you, scribes and Pharisees, hypocrites! For you are like whitewashed tombs, which outwardly appear beautiful, but within are full of dead people's bones and all uncleanness" (Matt. 23:27). The Pharisees performed religious duties, but overlooked what God cared about the most, the condition of the heart. External behavior did not match internal intentions. They failed to understand that behavior is linked to attitudes of the heart. Thus, Jesus called them hypocrites, because the irreligious behavior masked their wicked hearts.

So when Michelle and I discussed how we were going to address issues like instilling values, administering discipline, training, and correcting behavior, we decided to begin with the heart. We sought to unmask issues originating in Faith's heart in a loving, graceful, and biblical way so that her heart could be changed.

We knew that to expose deep issues of the heart, we must use several communication strategies. First of all, we sought to encourage Faith. Solomon was quite right when he said, "Hope deferred makes the heart sick" (Prov. 13:12). We wanted to instill in Faith a desire to obey God and to obey us but not have her fall in despair when she fails to obey. When she failed, we made it a practice to encourage her and continually reinforce our love for her. This would help her understand that heart change was something to seek, not to avoid. God does not reject His children when they come to Him; He longs for them to be in His presence. However, the only way to approach a holy God like Him, is to take the free grace He offers and enter His presence with total honesty about what is going on in the heart. We wanted Faith to learn this concept, and we taught it with intentionality.

Secondly, when we did need to correct her, we did so by addressing the issues of her heart. We really began this when Faith turned four-years-old. At four, her cognitive faculties had developed to a point that she could understand and communicate her heart. For example, we taught Faith to say she was sorry whenever she disobeyed us.

Typically, the scenario went like this. I would need to correct her. After I did, I would have her say, "Sorry, Daddy", or, "Sorry, Mommy." She would tilt her head downward, stick out her bottom lip as far it would go, then repeat what we said. By having her say these words, she began to understand that she had done wrong and needed to address that deeper issue of her heart's intent. She was really sorry for it and we could tell she wanted a clear relationship with us. Once she acknowledged her wrongdoing, I would pick her up and give her a big hug and a kiss on the cheek. She always responded with a big smile and a hug back. Correcting her this way helped her understand that discipline is a loving act by her parents for her good and the good of our relationship. By associating discipline with love, we hope to help Faith be honest with what is going on her heart in the future, not only with us, her earthly parents, but also with her heavenly Father.

Thirdly, we seek to instruct and teach Faith God's precepts. We do this in three ways.

One way we do this is we read Christian-oriented stories to Faith. When we go through a book, I allow her to ask the "What's that?" and "Who's that?" questions appropriate to those children her age ask. I tell her the names of the characters as we read and explain who they are. I hope she will be familiar with many of the characters as she grows older. While she may not comprehend the stories completely, she will be familiar with the biblical characters which will provide a building block for future learning.

Another way we teach and instruct Faith is to act out biblical stories. While I admit we don't do this as often as I would like, Faith enjoys helping with the stories, and this adds to her understanding quite a bit. We use props and toys to act out stories such as the David and Goliath story or Noah's Ark. These themes will become familiar to her, and she will be able to relate those elements to her knowledge as she grows in her understanding of God's word.

A final way we teach and instruct Faith is to take advantage of teachable moments. For example, Michelle likes to remind Faith the necessity of being thankful. As soon as Faith was able to sign "thank you" Michelle had her say the words whenever she could. If a friend gave her a toy, she had her say or sign, "Thank you." If an adult complimented her, she would prompt her to say, "Thank you". We model this as well by saying thank you to her and to each other. After a while, Michelle no longer needed to prompt her. It became a part of who she is. Now Michelle and I reap the benefits of such a thankful heart in Faith. If we bring her a drink or do any little thing for her, we get the delightful, heartfelt reply, "Thank you, Mommy", or "Thank you, Daddy." It warms our hearts just knowing our child is deeply thankful in her heart.

In the end, we hope to instill in Faith the resources to develop a solid understanding and lasting incorporation of the Christian faith. She will be so much closer to understanding the grace and love of God if we continue to raise her by protecting and nurturing her heart along with biblical correction as needed. Proverbs 22:6 says, "Train up a child in the way he should go; even when he is old he will not depart from it." As parents we eagerly strive to do this and believe Faith will benefit greatly as a result.

Develop a God Orientation

When I was a boy, my family came together at the dinner table to eat and talk about what happened during our day. It was a sacred time that didn't allow for disruptions like a television show or a sporting event. We all had to be at the dinner table ready to eat at 6 p.m.

Michelle and I were married for over sixteen years when we adopted Faith. Up until then, our meals were often eaten in the living room watching TV. When we adopted Faith, we decided to sit together and eat at the table when it was time for supper. One of our goals, of course, was to pray together before eating. We did this with Faith from the beginning, even before she could understand the meaning of prayer. When she was old enough, she folded her hands to pray, but she didn't say anything; normally, she would look down and smile, knowing we were focused on her and were inviting her to participate. Sometime around the age of four or five, that began to change. I would usually pray for the meal, but now Faith would ask to pray, too. She would say, "Faith pray," and would bow her head, exhort everyone else at the table to hold hands and bow their heads, and then she would begin to mouth some words. After about thirty seconds, she would say an enthusiastic "Amen" for a finale. She had learned through observation and much repetition that we should pray for our food and give thanks.

While these dinner prayers had value, we wanted her understanding of God to grow even deeper. Faith needed learn to know God personally. We want her to know that the God who created the universe wants a relationship with His creatures, and with her specifically. Jesus came to die and be raised again, so people would receive Him as Lord and Savior in order to have a relationship with God.

We help her by modeling what a person who loves God looks like. God has created children to be receptors. This means children are wired to be mentored. If you have ever traveled down South, you probably noticed the people native to the area talk with an accent. Words like "y'all" and "over yonder" are normal expressions. While the rest of the United States has regional differences in words and expressions, none are as famous as those from the South. How does one explain this? Do the people who live in the South take classes to learn to speak with such an accent? Of course not! They automatically learned it by living with and watching their parents talk. They automatically picked it up.

Michelle and I try to live an authentic Christian life before Faith. Authentic doesn't mean perfect, however. The Yahoo online dictionary defines authentic as "conforming to fact and therefore worthy of trust, reliance, or belief." I find this to be a very good definition, especially when living in Christian faith. This means what we profess to be in public, we should also be in private. The two lives must match. Many kids turn away from the faith because of hypocrisy, something Michelle and I always try to remember. We want our lives to reflect what we believe, so people, and most importantly Faith, will find us worthy of respect. Trust can then be rooted in family relationships, and it takes off the pressure of being someone you are not.

We must be honest about our faults and ask for forgiveness if we have done something wrong. If I raise my voice at Faith when she drops her drink on the floor, I should ask forgiveness and explain that I was wrong. I should use the words, "I'm sorry," just as I taught her to do with me. This is a verbal cue for her to understand the situation, put herself in my shoes, and realize we have a mutual relationship of love and forgiveness.

Develop a Gospel Orientation

As Christian parents, we want to foster something more than just belief in God. Mere belief in God does not make one a Christian. It is amazing that God's plan of salvation is reflected in the Trinity. The Father, the Son, and the Holy Spirit all comprise the Trinity. There is one God manifested in three persons. Each person of the Trinity is divine and each is involved in salvation (Eph. 1:3-14).

God the Father is the originator of salvation as He planned it in eternity past. He also oversees the process. Jesus came to save us. The Bible teaches that salvation is found in no one else. Jesus' life, death, burial, and resurrection provide the means of salvation. Through Christ, when people repent of their sins and trust Christ alone for salvation, they are justified before God and enter into a relationship with Him. God the Spirit plays the third role in salvation. God the Spirit, also called the Holy Spirit, draws people to God by convicting them of their sins and illuminating the plan of salvation to them. After conversion, the

Holy Spirit continues the salvation process by encouraging and convicting believers in order to make them more like Christ.

Parenting, for us, must be gospel-centered so we believe that our parenting should reflect the overall message of the Bible, including this amazing salvation message. Faith needs to know, as we all do, that a holy God seeks to reconcile sinful man to Himself. If we wish to be gospel-centered in our parenting, our goals must coincide with God's goals. Since God's essential goal is to reconcile sinful man to Himself, we must have the same goal in our parenting. We want Faith to come to Christ and accept Him as Savior and Lord. We also want her to be someone who lives out the faith authentically. These goals have shaped our parenting style tremendously.

As we parent Faith, we hope to help her deal biblically with the issues of her heart. In doing so, we hope to show her that she needs a Savior. Once she understands that her sin separates her from God, she will see the need to come to Christ for salvation. As Michelle and I model the love and grace of God, Faith will better understand how God extends that same love and grace to her.

Chapter 16

Faith Attends a New School

On July 17, 2014, Faith turned five-years-old, thereby entering the school-aged years. We celebrated this milestone with a birthday party with all her friends. Michelle organized all of the festivities such as the food, drink, and all of the games. We had the party at a local park with outdoor views of the lake and kids playing near the shelter. Everyone seemed to be enjoying the celebration immensely.

For Michelle and me, however, we celebrated much more than a birthday. One of the signs Michelle put up at the party told Faith how much we loved her and were so happy to be the parents of a young girl who was quickly growing up! This birthday signaled the end of phase one of Faith's development plan.

When Faith was very young we mapped out a plan for her growth. We decided to break it down in phases. Phase one began at birth and lasted until she entered kindergarten. Then phase two started when she began kindergarten and lasts until she finishes elementary school. When she begins middle school, she will enter into the last phase before adulthood, her high school experience ending in graduation.

Michelle and I are so thankful for the people who have assisted us in her development in phase one. We found that the social service agencies and the school worked together with us to educate Faith. Thanks to the *Individuals with Disabilities Act* originally titled *Education for All Handicapped Children Act*, a bill congress passed in 1975, children like Faith are guaranteed to receive the necessary service needed to develop as closely as possible to their same age peers.

We appealed to these agencies for their expert assistance. For the first three years of phase one, the *First Steps* program served Faith through a local company called *A Step Ahead*. The wonderful program included dedicated staff who assisted Faith with her occupational, physical, and speech therapy needs while at the same time educating us on Faith's development and needs.

At age three, Faith was no longer eligible to receive help from First Steps. Now, she would get help from the wonderful staff at Parkside Elementary School who took over the therapy responsibilities for Faith. Both organizations played an important role in Faith's physical and social development plan with the goal of preparing her for the ever important kindergarten year.

Taylorsville Elementary School

Faith began phase two of her life by attending a new school, Taylorsville Elementary. If you recall from previous chapters, Columbus Christian School helped us reach our scholastic goals for Faith, namely being involved in a learning community.

Faith will spend the next seven years attending elementary school. This means that Taylorsville will be her school for quite some time. To put it in perspective, a child spends seven hours a day in school for 183 days a year. That means he or she will spend 1,281 hours a year at school. When you multiply that number by seven years, a child will spend one full year at school. Like it or not, the school will play a part in shaping a child's future. Our top priority remained: having Faith in a learning community where she could flourish.

Faith's First Day

When Faith began her first day of school, I took her. As I entered the school, I first noticed the racial diversity. Some may not prefer to live in a diverse community, but I do. I had spent the majority of my life having many cross-cultural relationships. In junior high school and beyond, I had many friends who were non-white.

The same cross-cultural experience followed me when I entered into ministry and worked as an elementary teacher. My motivation for being in cross-cultural relationships was not strategic on my part but just seemed most comfortable to me. I would rather live in a culturally diverse city than live in a suburban situation lacking diversity. I believe being exposed to others from different ethnicities and backgrounds helps us learn to be more loving of all people as Christ teaches us to be. For that reason, I prefer having Faith attend a learning community that is racially diverse.

Michelle shared my desire to live in culturally diverse situations. Her chosen career path as a Spanish and ESL teacher reflected her love for and commitment to cultural diversity. She had also followed me to East Chicago to plant a church, which was one of the highlights of her life. So we were both excited that Faith would have the same multicultural experience that Michelle and I enjoyed.

A Learning Community

Even though I was thrilled that Faith had similar opportunities for cross-cultural relationships, the question still lingered in my mind: "Was Faith attending the right school where she could develop key skills that would be important to her future success?" Many attributes of Taylorsville Elementary assured me that Faith was in the right place.

Was this school an educational community? It might seem obvious to think that all schools are learning communities. School is naturally just a place you go to learn. I disagree. When I think of a learning community, borrowing from Ferdinand Tönnies, I think of a diverse group of people who work together to fulfill roles and embrace shared values and beliefs that serve to connect everyone to the community. I wanted this for Faith's educational experience.

Most schools tend to be learning societies, impersonal communities that develop and change based on the ebb and flow of the group. This society has no intentionality. In this model, status quo and management reign. In other words, it is a learning institution that doesn't intentionally seek to connect everyone to the community. The individual is expected to learn the society's ways to survive.

In a learning society, educating the students is the teacher's job, but there is no commitment for the school community as a whole to act as co-educators with the teacher. If the school meets the goals of standardized testing, then the school is seen as successful. However, if it is simply meeting the goals of test scores, and not developing a true sense of community, then a learning society is built, not a learning community.

In a true learning community, at least as I understand it, the community as a whole educates and relates with the child. The custodians, the secretaries in the office, support staff, and fellow teachers know each child, or at least seek to involve themselves into the community's educational process. Therefore, school leadership must work diligently to intentionally foster such a community.

When Faith entered kindergarten, she entered a new learning environment. Since we could no longer afford private school, Faith's sole educational experience would come from the public school system. We were concerned about whether Faith would now enter a learning society or a learning community.

Our first introduction to Faith's new school came by way of the Parkside Elementary's exit interview. In the interview, the Parkside staff explained to us that Taylorsville would assume all of Faith's therapy needs. The interview went extremely well and we all decided that Faith would be able to handle a full day at Taylorsville with minimal support. It was exciting to think that our little girl had spent two years preparing for this, and now she was ready for kindergarten!

However, we became a little anxious when they went on to explain the bussing options to us. If Faith rode the bus, she would not necessarily receive any special services as she had in the past. Her previous bus experiences were hand-to-hand delivery of Faith with direct care and supervision the whole way. Now she would have to be put on the bus by us, sit in the front of the bus, get off on her own and go into the building with the other students. We just could not envision our little Faith being able to do that, even with all of her advances. Now, the school made the decision whether they could accommodate Faith's needs in this area or not.

After discussing it with Michelle, I decided to call the principal, Mrs. Gant, about Faith's possible bus situation. I explained that Faith could not get off the bus by herself and I wasn't comfortable with having another student lead her to her class from the bus. To my surprise, she had already called the bus driver before I even had a chance to speak with her and had arranged for the driver to walk Faith into the school if need be. I took this as a sign that the principal and staff really understood the concept of a learning community.

Even with Mrs. Gant's kind offer, we decided it would be best for me to take Faith in to school that year. As I dropped Faith off the first few days of school, I noticed the person greeting everyone at the door knew Faith by name. A day or two later, I talked briefly with the same lady at the door where she shared with me the few interactions she had already had with Faith. She already knew Faith personally and had become familiar with her needs.

The next day, while walking Faith to the gym to drop her off, the custodian walked by and called Faith by name. He told me how he enjoyed interacting with her. The same was true with the office staff and the support staff. Within the first week, several staff members not only knew Faith, but seemed to care about her as well as her success as a student.

We also noticed that the teaching support staff took a personal interest in Faith. For example, a few days before Christmas break, the speech therapist, Mrs. Clapp, asked me if Michelle and I would be interested in a Christmas dress for Faith. She showed me the stunning dress, a red and plaid skirt with a beautiful white sweater that fit Faith perfectly. I told her that it was our tradition to attend Christmas Eve service every year, and Faith would definitely be wearing the dress on Christmas Eve.

These brief examples, illustrate that a learning community had been developed intentionally at Taylorsville Elementary. Not just Faith, but all the other students were receiving the same treatment. Each individual staff member played an integral part in meeting individual needs, establishing relational connections, and educating the child with the goal of fostering student success.

Educational Community

Of course, qualified teachers complete the well-rounded educational learning community.

Michelle and I first met Mrs. West, Faith's new kindergarten teacher, shortly before the school year began. Young and energetic, probably in her late twenties or early thirties, she had confidence in what she did. As we entered into the classroom, her organization did not escape our notice. The axiom often quoted regarding planning says, "Failing to plan, is planning to fail." Conversely, then, deciding to plan is deciding to succeed. Based on first impressions, Mrs. West did her job well and planned for all of her students to succeed. This brought further comfort to Michelle and me.

Our first impression was confirmed many times over. For example, we learned that Mrs. West had a genuine love and concern for her students, evident when within the first few weeks she emailed us almost daily about Faith's progress as well as some skills we may need to work on with her. This made the transition to kindergarten a smoother one because

Faith struggled at first, and this information helped us all give Faith the support she needed.

As the year went on, we noticed how much Faith was learning. She said new phrases almost daily, identified letter sounds, and even began to sound out words. She already knew her alphabet from preschool, and we knew Faith had a solid foundation in language arts. However, we were concerned with math and numbers.

Her class was working hard on learning to count to 100 in order to celebrate 100 days of school. While preparing for the big day, Faith was helping Michelle count 100 stamps she was planning to take to school the next day. To Michelle's and my surprise, Faith started counting along by tens! Seeing our reaction let her know this was a pretty big deal. Her facial expressions in response told the whole story.

On another occasion, I was walking down the aisle at the grocery store as Faith was sitting in the child's seat of the shopping cart. Usually she wants to coach me on what to buy, especially when we travel down the cereal aisle. But this time was different. She started counting the boxes in order way beyond twenty. I knew she didn't get it from me since we had only been practicing up to around twenty at home. For a child with her disability, she excelled beyond many people's expectations. The reason for her success went beyond home learning. The school contributed to a large part of her learning.

School Leadership

I was excited by what I had already seen. The last question I needed an answer to was, "Could all of this success be sustained over time?" The affirmative answer to that question came once I got to know and observe the principal lead. Years ago, I heard John Maxwell say that everything rises and falls on leadership. For a learning community to be effective over the long term requires strong leadership.

When I met Mrs. Gant for the first time, I noticed she was probably in her mid to late thirties, very energetic, and seemed to be on top of things. I later discovered that her engaging and kind personality transferred not only to parents but to the students and staff the same way.

After the school year began, I spent time at the school and saw her leadership firsthand. I was very impressed by what I saw. What determines future success is the ability to hire, retain, and train excellent teachers. As I served within the school and observed the quality staff that worked there, I knew this strong leadership would continue to sustain an effective learning community. After all, the principal has excellent people skills and a unique ability to build strong relationships with students, staff and parents, which goes a long way to further continued success.

Conclusion

Though parental support remains vital for student success, it will have limited impact without a strong educational institution. This is why educators work diligently to create successful learning environments. Investing in well-educated children ensures a bright future. We look forward to seeing what phase two at Taylorsville will bring to our daughter; Faith's future looks bright to me.

Chapter 17

Faith: A Vision for Her Future

H ave you ever been to a Little League game and watched a driven father live vicariously through his son attempting to achieve the dream of baseball prominence that he was unable to achieve as a boy? The father drives his son to achieve baseball greatness that is really beyond the poor kid's skill level. He sits in the stands and yells at his son when he drops a ball or doesn't make a play. The conversation on the way home revolves around the son's performance in the game where shame and anger are used to motivate the son to play better next time. The father fails to entertain the idea that his son might be doing the best he can. Instead of letting him discover his limits, he sets up limits beyond his capability. The father is not happy even when the son tries his best.

Attainable Goals

Michelle and I don't want to be the kind of parents who set unattainable goals. We just want Faith to reach her full potential as a woman, nothing more and nothing less. We do not want to apply pressure in order to reach some predetermined goal. We want her to do her best and realize whatever limitations she might have on her own; we don't want to set any limits for her.

Beginning with the End in Mind

In order to convey our plan for Faith to reach her full potential, I will hearken back to a time in my life to illustrate how and why we formulated our plan.

In December 1999, over fifteen years ago now, I walked down the aisle to receive my first college diploma. It had been a tough road. My high school experience was a rough one. I graduated with the third lowest grade point average in my graduating class. About a month before graduation, my school counselor called me into her office and informed me that I might not graduate. The thought hit like a brick. I was one of the low achieving students. Some in my graduating class took longer than four years to graduate because they did not have enough credits to do so. I realized that I might be one of those students.

Academics never came easy for me growing up. Today, people are shocked when they hear me say that because people see me as an academic. Truly, this has not always been the case. From the third grade on, I never did well in school. I didn't lack the intelligence needed to succeed, just the personal discipline to do so.

I entered college in 1991, two years after my conversion, and didn't do well there either. I arrived at Lee University with high hopes. Realistically, I never thought I would ever go to college, but my dream to do so had arrived. During my first week, when the school tested my reading proficiency, they found it to be at a ninth grade level. In spite of this, I was determined to succeed. By the end of the first year, my reading level was that of a freshman in college after much hard work.

Unfortunately, my grades were not congruent with my rise in reading comprehension. I struggled very much with my course work. Growing up, I had never developed good study habits and had a very difficult time comprehending what I read. I ended up leaving Lee University, which was then Lee College, during the middle of my second year with a grade point average of below 2.0.

After sitting out three years from college, I enrolled at one of the campuses of Indiana University. One of the admission counselors, after looking at my prior academic record, suggested that I take a study skills course. The course revolutionized my academic career. I learned in that class what most middle class students learn from their parents, namely the study skills to make them successful students.

The professor taught us to begin with the end in mind. She instructed us to visualize walking down the aisle with a diploma in hand. This suggestion was followed by another one: writing down what it will take to accomplish this goal. So I did. I formulated a plan to reach the goal of graduation.

This exercise encouraged students to do what Stephen Covey suggested in his book, *Seven Habits of Highly Effective People*, to begin with the end in mind. Covey called for people to see in the future what is not evident currently. I had just begun to see the possibilities, but the goal was four years into the future. That day in the classroom, I put a plan in place which would lead to achieving my goal. In other words, I accomplished the goal by first looking to the end result and planning backward.

Michelle and I applied the same reasoning to Faith's remaining academic career. We wanted her to acquire the needed skills to communicate with her peers, read books, do basic math, and eventually live on her own.

For me, I sought to develop a mental conception of Faith's future. I asked myself questions like, "Would she be able to read, write, or relate well with her peers?" Taking my cue from Covey, I formulated my goals for Faith by looking to what I saw as reasonable goals for her as she finishes her sixth grade year.

Stage Two Begins

A few hours after Faith came into the world, we began our journey with her. We had a short stabilization period where Faith stayed at the hospital for first two months of her life.

We now embarked on our parenthood journey. God had entrusted this new little girl into our care. Today we look back and feel so fortunate for the all of Faith's progress. We watched her learn how to sit up, walk and talk, exhibiting great efforts to do so. It wasn't easy for her, but her tenacity augmented by God's sovereign hand working in her life, helped her to make these strides.

Now phase two of her life has begun. We had the obvious parental concerns because the gap between a typical child and a child with Down syndrome typically widens during this period, far more than is the case in phase one. Questions obviously emerged in our minds. Questions like, "Would Faith make the same strides in the next seven years as she did the first five?", or "Would the widening gap of her classmates discourage her?" Initially, she succeeded in part because, after much effort, she could keep up, relatively speaking, with the rest of her classmates. Now, as the next few years ensue, she will likely fall further and further behind. Her limitations will be increasingly obvious even to her.

Despite this widening gap intellectually, we are persuaded that Faith will more than make up for that gap socially. It wouldn't surprise me if she is one of the most popular girls in her class for years to come. She has a God-given way about her with the skill to connect with people. I have observed already that her classmates not only like her, but her leadership skills have been obvious as many of them look up to her. She seems to have natural leadership capabilities. This will take her very far in her life.

Casting a Vision for Faith's Future

To cast a vision for her future, we began by looking at the possibilities through the lens of other people with Faith's disability. We hope to help Faith fulfill the full God-given potential for her life. If she is able to live on her own one day, relatively speaking, we hope that she will be able to do that. If she is able to get married one day, I look forward to walking her down the aisle and watching her marry the man of her dreams. For her to accomplish these goals, we still have work to do. When she becomes an adult and is not able to do some of those things, that is okay, too. We just want to see her live the life God intended for her.

Possibly by the age of twenty-one or so, Faith may be at the point where she is able to live alone with some assistance. That day for us will not be an easy one. Through parenting, we have built a strong bond. We have spent years developing emotional ties, trust, and love for one another. The times spent vacationing together, wiping Faith's tears when she hurts, taking care of her when she is sick, and the quality time having face-to-face talks all combine to form these ties. Like most parents, we have a strong parent/child bond. By the time she is ready to go out on her own, the bonding will have grown even deeper.

As Christians, parenting is also stewardship. If she lives on her own one day, we know that God entrusted Faith to our care for a reason, with the purpose of raising her to be an adult who brings Him glory. While she will always be our daughter, she won't always be our little girl. If she is able to attain this goal, Michelle and I want her to live on her own. We want her to make her own decisions, cook her own food, wash her own dishes and pay her own bills. We pray she will experience the joy of living independently without having to depend on mom and dad all of the time. This may mean living in an apartment we create for her in our home, like a basement apartment, or it may mean some other living arrangement. Only time will tell. We will encourage her to live on her own if she is able.

As Christians, we believe that God created people in His image. This means that human beings have essential dignity. The term also means, as the British theologian N. T. Wright wisely states, that humans are the bearers of God's image and have the capacity to reflect back to the world His love, care, and stewardship in the same manner God has reflected those qualities to humankind.[14] If we limited Faith in experiencing life to the fullest, we would limit her usefulness to God in reflecting His glory to the world. What could be a better testimony and reflection of God's glory than to see someone with Faith's disability live a successful life because of His faithfulness?

I struggle with the question of Faith getting married. Since Faith is only five, it seems odd to even think about such a thing. In my heart, I want her to be daddy's little girl forever. However, I want her to enjoy everything Michelle and I have

---

[14] N. T. Wright https://www.youtube.com/watch?v=yp-Ku-_ekAY accessed on March 9, 2015

had the pleasure to experience in our marriage, especially companionship and love. If she is able to do so, we want her to experience it.

Fortunately for Faith, her mom will be a very good mentor for her when that time comes. Each day Faith is learning from someone who loves her husband and daughter and puts their needs before her own. This example, together with the life skills that she will learn along the way, will help prepare her for marriage if that time comes. We pray that as Faith observes our marriage, she will find a blueprint for hers.

Working Backward

Faith must work very hard to master certain skills today in order to accomplish those goals. With each skill, she lays a building block for the future. To communicate with people, she will need speech. To shop for groceries, she will need the math skills appropriate for the task. To write a note or read directions, she will need to be proficient in the English language. This will take a group effort between home and school. Faith will meet these goals with all of our help. We will first seek God's mind and heart on raising our child, look for opportunities to nurture her growth both academically and spiritually and never put limits on what she can do.

Final Thoughts

Michelle and I look forward to watching Faith grow up the next several years. Until five years ago, we never thought we would have the chance to raise a daughter of our own. But God had other plans. He placed Faith into our care for a purpose, a divine one indeed. We consider it an honor and a privilege that God has allowed us to join Him in shaping Faith's life so she can fulfill God's plan.

God indeed has a plan for each of His children. The often quoted passage in Jeremiah reflects God's heart for his people. Jeremiah 29:11 declares, "For I know the plans I have for you, declares the LORD, plans ... to give you a future and a hope."

In our world, as has been the case since the fall of man, the mighty are honored and the seemingly lowly are not. God had great plans for men and women like Billy Graham, John Piper, and Nancy Leigh DeMoss. These great people have impacted the world through their ministry.

God also has great plans for the many men and women we will never know by name. God doesn't operate on human terms. God has a plan for each one of His children. Sometimes He uses well-known people to reveal His plan on a grand scale. Most people, however, God uses in smaller ways. Not many people know what they do for God. That is the way God intended. After all, He is sovereign. He will exalt the ones He wishes to exalt, all for the purpose of bringing Him glory.

While He does give everyone the same gifts, God is just, and because of this, He does not show favoritism among his people. God's plan for Faith's life remains just as important to Him as His plan for Graham, Piper, and DeMoss. God is no respecter of persons.

He constructed his plan for Faith before time began. His plan for Michelle and me was also constructed before time. God is not surprised by anything that has taken place. He knew that I would be born in the condition I was born. He knew of the operations, He knew of the rejection, and He knew all about my family situation. God used all of these experiences to form me into the person that I am so I could be used to minister to Faith and be the father He wanted me to be.

As for Michelle, God knew the infertility battle that she would endure. He understood the longing in her heart to be a mother. God used that longing to minister to kids during the early years of our ministry, and he used it to compel her desire to adopt Faith. This was His way of guiding the process. We are grateful that God used our experiences as a tool to assist Him.

The Bible uses the metaphor of a hand to describe His work in the lives of His people. Now God doesn't have a literal hand, of course. Throughout Scripture the image of His hand is used to show how God moves, guides, disciplines and directs His people. He protects them from harm, orders their steps, and allows events in their lives that will lead them to trust in Him.

The historian uses forensic analysis to determine what has taken place in the past.

Similarly, the Christian can look at what has transpired in the past to determine how God has moved in his or her life. What I have hoped to communicate in this book is a forensic analysis of the life and experiences of Michelle, Faith and me to tell a story about our little girl and how God brought us all three together to bring Him glory and create a gospel-centered family.

We are grateful to God for what he has done already and excited about what we believe He will do in the future. He has good plans, and He will reveal them through the coming years.

As I finish this book, I am sitting down at my desk, watching Faith play with her toys. She is intent on building a house with her Lego set. One day she will trade that set in for a bike and something more sophisticated after that. Until then, Michelle and I will enjoy the privilege of watching Faith learn and grow from our little daughter into a woman of God.

Bibliography

Duncan, Ligon. "Male Authority and Female Equality: In the beginning—Genesis 1-3 being understood as part of God's created design". *Council on Biblical Manhood and Womanhood.*

http://dictionary.reference.com/browse/gemein-schaft http://listverse.com/2012/05/07/top-10-famous-mothers-and-their-daughters/

http://www.searchquotes.com/quotation/A_daughter_ needs_a_loving%2C_available%2C_predic table_father_or_father_figure_who_can_be_counted_ on%2C_whe/278035/ retrieved on March 9, 2015

Khurana, Simran. "21 Sweet Father's Day Quotes from Daughters to Dads." About Education.

2015. http://quotations.about.com/od/happyfathersday-quotes/a/Fathers-Day-Quotes- From-Daughter.htm

Miller, J.R. *Secrets of a Happy Home Life*. Bottom of the Hill Publishing, 2011.

Parnell, Jonathan. "God Will Fulfill His Purpose for You." *Desiring God*. 14 December 2014. http://www.desiringgod.org/blog/posts/god-will-fulfill-his-purpose-for-you

Pearsey, Nancy. *Total Truth: Liberating Christianity from its Cultural Captivity*. Wheaton, IL: Crossway, 2008

"Social Development for Individuals with Down Syndrome." *Down Syndrome Education Online*. 2014. http://www.down-syndrome.org/information/social/overview/?page=4

Tripp, Ted. Shepherding a Child's Heart. INSERT place – name of city- of Publication here: Shepherd Press, 1995.

Winders, Patricia C. "Physical Therapy & Down Syndrome." *National Down Syndrome Society*. 2012. http://www.ndss.org/Resources/Therapies-Development/Physical- Therapy-Down-Syndrome/

Wright, N. T. https://www.youtube.com/watch?v=yp-Ku-_ekAY

About the Author

Tim Orr is an award winning adjunct faculty member in Religious Studies for teaching excellence at Indiana University Purdue Columbus where he has served for over 7 years. He holds three Master degrees and is currently finishing his Doctorate degree. His dramatic conversion and subsequent life change has been featured on the Pat Robertson's *700 Club*. Tim has served as a pastor, church planter, elder, and also has a heart for building bridges with the Muslim community. His greatest joy in life, however, is being a husband to Michelle and a father to Faith.

CPSIA information can be obtained at www.ICGtesting.com
Printed in the USA
BVOW11s0507221015

423456BV00009B/45/P

9 781498 431613